Sign Me Alice
& Laurent Clerc:
A Profile

by Gilbert C. Eastman

Sign Me Alice & Laurent Clerc: A Profile—Two Deaf Plays
Copyright ©1974, Gilbert C. Eastman

Printed in the United States of America.
Published by DawnSignPress

Library of Congress Cataloging-in-Publication Data

Eastman, Gilbert C.
    [Sign me Alice]
    Sign me Alice ; and, Laurent Clerc : a profile / by Gilbert C. Eastman.
        p.   cm.
    ISBN 0-915035-60-X (alk. paper)
        1. Clerc, Laurent, 1785-1869—Drama.   2. Teachers of the deaf—Drama.
3. Deaf—Drama. I. Eastman, Gilbert C. Laurent Clerc. II. Title. III. Title: Laurent
Clerc.
PS3555.A717S5   1997
812' . 54—dc21

                                                            97-3642
                                                                CIP

                    10   9   8   7   6   5   4   3   2   1

ATTENTION: SCHOOLS & DISTRIBUTORS

Quantity discounts for schools and bookstores are available.
For information, please contact:

DAWNSIGNPRESS
6130 Nancy Ridge Drive
San Diego, CA 92121-3223
619-625-0600 V/TTY 619-625-2336 FAX
ORDER TOLL FREE 1-800-549-5350

To June with love

I was never taught sign language
but it grew in my heart
and led me
to seek the truth,
to find the truth,
to speak the truth
and live the truth.

Gilbert C. Eastman

TABLE OF CONTENTS

Sign Me
Alice

FOREWORD

Long ago, there was a time when Latin was the name all over Europe for language; but every region had its own "vernacular", and how you spoke it depended on whether you were a priest or peasant, common soldier or aristocratic officer. That time ended when Dante presented to the world—not in Latin but in the Italian vernacular—his *Commedia*.

Not long after, there was a time when the ruling classes in England spoke French—out of Normandy; and the common people they ruled over used some dialect or other of Anglian or Saxon origin. That time of division ended too, and no one man helped times and customs change more than did Chaucer, who took the styles of speech of high and low alike and shaped them into the human comedy of his *Canterbury Tales*.

Just lately there was a time when the deaf people of America who loved their "beautiful language of signs" bequeathed to them by Abbe de l'Epee and Sicard through the teaching of Gallaudet and Clerc, found that in return for a chance at education, they must renounce their inheritance and give lip service to the credo that only English "has grammar" and "is a language." Happily we are alive to see this time ending and the dawn of a new golden age of the deaf. *Sign Me Alice* is a delightful comedy. It is an affirmation too, that language used naturally need not fit fusty pedantic definitions of it to be a real language. By writing this play and by writing it in American Sign Language, Gilbert Eastman has joined an illustrious company of originators.

William C. Stokoe, Jr.

FROM THE PLAYWRIGHT

Sign Me Alice is my first attempt at writing a play; it is based on George Bernard Shaw's *Pygmalion* as was Alan Jay Lerner's *My Fair Lady*. I have no intention of copying the Shavian style or Lerner's musical numbers. The names of the characters, the locations and the period of the story are completely different but the problems of the language are somewhat parallel. I have borrowed some lines from both plays.

In the past years the Gallaudet University Theatre has presented classic or contemporary plays in which the principal characters (antagonist and protagonists) express their ideas, arguments, and feelings in speeches that must be translated, and we the deaf don't fully live the parts because they portray the life of the hearing.

Sign Me Alice is about the life of the deaf mingling in the world of the hearing. The heroine does not ask for pity but for the right to the deaf's choice: sign language.

Never before have I written a play in American Sign Language, and now I face the difficulty of presenting the signs in English words. The reader may find the speeches strange to read, but a system of representing signs in different print shows important differences in actual performance. A table of word-codes for signs appears on page 3.

If you intend to produce this play, it is advisable to have a deaf consultant who is familiar with the different artificial languages and with varieties of true sign language.

Gilbert C. Eastman

INTRODUCTION

The production of *Sign Me Alice* marked a high point, if not a culmination, for its author and for the Gallaudet University Theatre. For fifteen years, Eastman and his Drama Department had been growing more professional in technique and outlook, exploring more fully the possibilities of their own talents. Graduates of the University staffed the new National Theatre of the Deaf, the two Little Theatres of the Deaf, and appeared with increasing frequency on film and in television. Productions of the GCT grew steadily in artistic assurance. In the 1972-73 season, its version of *Antigone*—as conceived, translated, and directed by Eastman—was sent to the Kennedy Center by the American College Theatre Festival, one of ten productions in a field of 312 to be so honored.

Theatrically speaking, it was a great year. But *Sign Me Alice* capped the year. It was the most popular play ever shown at Gallaudet; it had the longest run, the largest audience, the greatest critical acclaim.

The reason for this popularity is not hard to define. It was a comedy, and audiences are supposed to prefer comedy. But much more important than that, it did everything that a comedy is supposed to do. For the first time in their lives, deaf audiences were shown a play about deaf people (and in the variety of languages that deaf people use today), in their characteristic confrontation with the "hearing" world over styles of communication, and the rewards that society offers to those who use the accepted style.

All of this was wrapped in an ingenious comic plot, a romantic sub-plot, and delivered with enormous grace and assurance by an attractive company of actors working in a magically shifting set.

It was irresistible. It was "in." It was even daring, because it challenged the doctrine that deaf people had been given in childhood and exposed it to laughter, the most destructive treatment possible.

The people who saw the play will never forget it; their lives were changed. They learned something. The function of comedy is to teach; and what it teaches is the most valuable lesson of all: how to know a fool when we see one; how to recognize foolish behavior.

The fools in the play are everywhere. They range from the extreme foolishness of Professor Zeno (who has invented a new sign language so much

1

like English that its users are promised all the social rewards given to English-speaking people) to the innocent foolishness of Mark, so much under the domination of his mother that he has become her vehicle for demonstrating Cued Speech. All the fools are marked for us by Alice. She may be poor, and at times confused by the conflicting claims for her ambition and affection; but her common-sense never deserts her. When she stands up to one of the foolish people, she is instantly exposed for what she is.

She is generous, kind in all her intentions; there is no malice in her. Nor is there malice in the play. Simple laughter is enough to cure the most outrageously ridiculous behavior. Even Professor Zeno is laughed into good sense at the end.

The present edition is prepared for those who have not seen the play, who—having seen it—wish to retain some record of it. Notes on the language and characters, as well as floor plans for the set, will help anyone who wishes to produce it again (the author's permission should be secured for such a production). All readers are warned that a play is meant to be performed and witnessed, not read. They are further warned that a comedy is the most ephemeral kind of play. It lives in the jokes and controversies of the moment; when they are forgotten, much of the humor departs. Research will restore understanding but not laughter.

Finally, this particular comedy was performed in a number of modes: in sign language, in an artificial language called by the playwright Using Signed English, in Cued Speech and in various mouthings—all of which are imperfectly rendered by English language script. Eastman has patiently distinguished the separate modes, so that the actor will know what to do at every point, and the reader will at least know what is going on. The play makes clear sense as an English script; but the thousand little jokes, puns, and word-plays are missing, as well as the lyric beauty of some passages, if the play is read simply as English.

When all warnings are given, however, the play remains a notable contribution to dramatic literature; a deaf playwright looks at the absurdities visited upon and created by the deaf people of his society.

George E. Detmold
Professor of Drama
Gallaudet University

2

WORD-CODES FOR SIGNS

word .... sign of American Sign Language (ASL)

<u>w</u>ord .... sign with letter

<u>word</u> .... fingerspelled

word-word .... one sign

word/word .... repeated sign

word=word .... same sign, both hands

word+word .... different sign each hand

WO\|RD .... gesture (generally understood)

"word" .... spoken word

[word] .... action or mime,
conventional state directions

*<u>n</u>ame .... sign for proper name

(S.C.) .... simultaneous communication

3

SIGN VOCABULARY

Special Signs

OH (Y)
Move Y several times

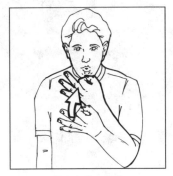

Can-do (9)
Place 9 on chin

CCC
C Handshape, crooked fingers,
facing head moving back-and-forth

Signs Used by Dr. Zeno Only

<u>t</u>his
Place <u>T</u> on palm

<u>t</u>hat
Place <u>T</u> forward

<u>t</u>hese
Place <u>T</u> on open palm, begin at
thumb and move to last finger

<u>t</u>hose
Place <u>T</u> forward,
move right

Proper Names

Chuck
Place <u>C</u> on chest

Mark
Place <u>M</u> on chin

Susie
Place <u>S</u> on cheek

Alice
Place <u>A</u> on cheek

Suggestions

MRS. PARHAM............... Stutters in signing

MISS MAUGHAN............... Use simultaneous communication

DR. ZENO............... Use <u>U</u>.<u>S</u>.<u>E</u>. with mouthing

Note: Initialized signs are based on American Manual Alphabet on the following page.

Initialized Signs in American Manual Alphabet

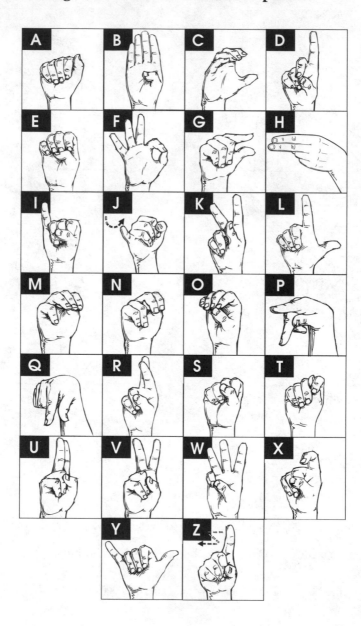

CAST OF ORIGINAL PERFORMANCE

Sign Me Alice was first presented by the Gallaudet University Theatre at the Gallaudet Auditorium, Kendall Green, Washington, D.C., April 6, 1973 with the following cast:

ALICE BABEL	Hedy Udkovich
DR. ALBERT ZENO	Steven Turner
DR. YLVISAKER	Matt Searls
MRS. PARHAM	Mary Ann Schoenberg
MISS MAUGHAN	Ella Lentz
MRS. NEWTON	Linda Hatrak
MARK NEWTON	Robert McMahon
MISS McCAIN	Donna Eads
VITO	Isaac Abenchuchan
TERRY	Douglas Bahl
CHUCK	Scott Kramer
PETE	Alan Barwiolek
SUSIE SLADE	Anna Zuccaro
THE FIRST LADY	Betsey-Freya Kaplan
HOTEL BELLBOY	Mineo Hoshina
HOTEL JANITOR	Norman Ingram
HOTEL CHAMBERMAID	Marilyn Nixon
EXTRAS	Jim Degnan
	Rosetta Duren
	Richard Garbacz
	Linda Herenchak
	Eugene LaCosse
	Ilene Liebman
	Reba Poole
	John Sigurdson

Directed by *Gilbert C. Eastman*
Designed and Lighting by *Jeffrey J. Grandel*

ACT I: SCENE 1

SCENE:
The lobby of the Pilgrim Hotel in Washington, DC in the afternoon in late October
after the convention. Center right is a bellboy desk with telephone. Downstage
right leads to the front of the hotel (not visible). Downstage left are a small couch,
an easy chair and a coffee table with magazines and newspapers. Center left leads
to the cocktail lounge (not visible). Upstage is a stairway (four steps) leading off left
and right. Up left is the convention room and upright the coffee shop and elevators
(neither are visible).

OPENING, ON THE STAGE:
BELLBOY at the desk, talking with MAID. GENTLEMAN sits on the couch, reading
a magazine. ALICE, a convention usherette, enters from the convention room, upleft,
carrying an empty tray and exits to the cocktail lounge, centerleft. TERRY, a
convention usher, enters upleft, crossing to the desk. CONVENTION DELEGATES
and ATTENDANTS enter upleft, pouring in and scattering in different directions.
TERRY distributes programs to some people. MAID leaves unnoticed, exits to the
cocktail lounge, left. DEAF ORALIST DELEGATE tries oral-speaking with one of
the deaf people who does not understand him and points at the BELLBOY. He goes
to BELLBOY, speaking but he does not understand and makes a gesture of "go-over-
there". He walks off to the hotel front, right. DEAF MANUALIST DELEGATE
writes on a pad, hands it to BELLBOY who then reads and nods repeatedly, dials the
phone and speaks to give a message for him, and then hangs up the phone and
makes a gesture of "OK". DEAF MANUALIST DELEGATE thanks him, exits right
to the hotel. DEAF FINGERSPELLING DELEGATES are upset by the recent debate
at the convention, move fingers rapidly to each other as they walk down, exit
downright. HEARING FAT LADY enters from the coffee shop, upright, looking for
someone, looks bewildered and then exits downright. HEARING CONVENTION
SECRETARY enters up left, walks straight to the desk and picks up the phone, dials
and waits for an answer. HEARING NEW HOTEL GUEST WOMAN with a suitcase
arrives from the hotel front, downright, stops at the desk. TWO DEAF DELEGATES
(a man and a young woman) enter upleft, signing about the convention. BELLBOY
takes HOTEL GUEST WOMAN'S suitcase, guides her upstage but she stops, staring
at DEAF DELEGATE's flying hands. BELLBOY calls to her to go upstairs and she
follows him. Both exit upright. DEAF YOUNG WOMAN DELEGATE exits
downright and DEAF MAN DELEGATE sits in the easy chair. GENTLEMAN at the

couch asks DEAF MAN DELEGATE in gestures "What time is it?" HEARING CHAIRMAN of the convention comes in upleft, rushes to CONVENTION SECRETARY who is still on the phone. HEARING FAT LADY re-enters downstage, stops at the desk and finds no BELLBOY. She keeps on looking for someone, exits to the cocktail lounge, center left. DEAF MAN enters from the hotel front, downright, recognizes DEAF MAN DELEGATE at the chair and walks to him and taps his shoulder. DEAF MAN DELEGATE looks up, rises, and offers hand to him. Both shake hands, signing rapidly. GENTLEMAN at the couch stares at them. Being disturbed by his behavior, they walk off to the cocktail lounge. CHAIRMAN at the desk gives some last-minute notes to CONVENTION SECRETARY and walks to the convention room. HEARING WOMAN DELEGATE enters from the coffee shop, running to CHAIRMAN and giving him some papers and both exit upleft. DEAF WOMAN DELEGATE re-enters downright, looking for someone and sees HEARING FAT LADY entering from the cocktail lounge left and walks to her. Both talk orally and then exit to the coffee shop upright. BELLBOY re-enters upright, returns to the desk. VITO, another convention usher, enters upleft, going to TERRY at the desk. ALICE with a tray of glasses re-enters from the cocktail lounge, goes to the upstage stairway. MARK NEWTON enters from the convention room, goes to the stairway. ALICE and MARK collide at the stairway; MARK strikes ALICE and the tray is knocked from her hands and the glasses scatter about. ALICE falls down on the lobby floor. The action is frozen for a few seconds and then MARK, TERRY, VITO, BELLBOY and GENTLEMAN run to her.

ALICE: [*Tries to rise*] CCC <u>Hurt</u>.

MARK: Sorry. Sorry.

ALICE: Look. You pushed me. For for. Watch, not look-up.

[*DR. YLVISAKER, Author of North America Indian Sign Language, enters from the convention room, sees ALICE on the floor and runs to her.*]

DR. YLVISAKER: <u>Are</u> you all-right?

ALICE: <u>Ok</u>. <u>Ok</u>. Man pushed me. Disgusted.

[*MRS. NEWTON, a social worker with the deaf and mother of MARK, enters from the convention room, sees MARK and DR. YLVISAKER helping ALICE to the chair. MRS. NEWTON crosses to MARK.*]

DR. YLVISAKER: <u>Are</u> you hurt?

ALICE: <u>No No</u>. Nothing.

MARK: Sorry. Real sorry.

MRS. NEWTON: [*to MARK*] <u>H</u>urry. <u>D</u>o you <u>w</u>ant me to <u>m</u>iss my <u>a</u>ppoint<u>m</u>ent?

MARK: Sorry. <u>I</u> <u>a</u>m <u>s</u>orry. <u>I</u> will drive you <u>r</u>ight away. [*to ALICE*] Real sorry real. *[to MRS. NEWTON]* <u>I</u> <u>a</u>m getti<u>n</u>g <u>t</u>he car. [*Exits downright*]

[*BELLBOY takes some papers from the desk, exits downright*]

ALICE: [*Rises from the chair, walks to MRS. NEWTON*] He your son?

MRS. NEWTON: Slow slow (*S.C.*) You <u>s</u>ign to<u>o</u> <u>f</u>ast.

ALICE: Your duty same all mothers . . .

MRS. NEWTON: Yes.

ALICE: You don't-want your son careless.

MRS. NEWTON: Yes

ALICE: What I said.

MRS. NEWTON: Yes.

ALICE: Hit girl like me.

MRS. NEWTON: Who?

ALICE: Now he ran-away.

MRS. NEWTON: Ran ed a way. (*S.C.*) "<u>O</u>h, <u>d</u>ear, that is terrible. Why <u>d</u>on't you <u>r</u>eport <u>i</u>t to <u>t</u>he <u>hotel</u> <u>m</u>anag<u>er</u>.

ALICE: You not understand.

MRS. NEWTON: Yes. <u>E</u>xcuse me. <u>I</u> ha<u>v</u>e to <u>g</u>o.

ALICE: CCC. She not understand me. [*Returns to the chair and sits, checking her leg.*]

DR. YLVISAKER: <u>Do</u> you want <u>to</u> go to my room and . . .

ALICE: <u>No</u> thank-you. NO NO NO.

DR. YLVISAKER: All I meant <u>was</u>, <u>do</u> you want <u>to</u> come to my room and let me . . .

ALICE: <u>No</u>. NO NO.

DR. YLVISAKER: <u>Are</u> you <u>sure</u>?

ALICE: Yes. Thank-you. You deaf?

DR. YLVISAKER: Yes . . . deaf like you . . . [*Smiles*] If you don't feel good, I'll <u>be</u> happy <u>to</u> help you. I will <u>be</u> around. BYE. [*Exits to the cocktail lounge.*]

ALICE: CCC

VITO: Be-careful. Better leave here now.

ALICE: Why. He helped me. Nice. He-left.

VITO: Look. I think cop look/look.

ALICE: Cop?

VITO: I mean <u>d</u>etective. He here [*Points at the man behind the column upstage.*] He look/look you. Has book taking-down everything he saw happen/happen.

ALICE: Nothing wrong. I not <u>do</u> anything. Nothing talking to man gentle. I nice girl. Really/really <u>d</u>etective here. Please help me. Don't-want trouble. Real not my fault. That man asked me go to his room. I said <u>no</u>. I won't.

MISS McCAIN: What <u>is</u> bothering her. What has happened?

VITO: Trouble. <u>D</u>etective [*Points at the man*]

MISS McCAIN: Don't point.

VITO: He stare/stare-at girl. She worried.

MISS McCAIN: Nothing new. Hearings always stare. Never saw deaf before. I sick.

ALICE: [*to TERRY*] Get my coat. I leave now.

14

[*TERRY runs and exits upleft.*]

VITO: Can't. Have-to wait for <u>C</u>huck.

ALICE: He should-be here. Always late=late. Really wrong time. Brought <u>tray</u> my last <u>job</u>. Everything went-smooth. That boy careless bumped . . .

MISS McCAIN: Who that boy?

ALICE: I don't-know.

MISS McCAIN: Deaf? Hearing?

ALICE: I don't-know. He left, ignore me. I fell-down right-here. Everybody looked-at-me. Really embarrassed.

VITO: Smart. Try get attention. Smart you.

ALICE: [*Gets mad*] Finish. Not true. You know-that.

[*TERRY re-enters with ALICE's coat*]

TERRY: Chairman beard just told me he will come and give us <u>paychecks</u>. Then we can leave.

ALICE: <u>C</u>huck <u>C</u>huck Where <u>C</u>huck

VITO: <u>B</u>e patient.

[*DR. YLVISAKER re-enters from the cocktail lounge, goes to the stairway. ALICE sees him, runs to him.*]

ALICE: Excuse me. I don't-want trouble. Man over-there stare/stare-at me. You not understand. He suspect me flirt you.

[*DR. ZENO, Author of Using Signed English, appears, walks down the stairway.*]

DR. ZENO: Hold on. Hold on. <u>W</u>hat <u>is</u> <u>b</u>othering you, you <u>s</u>illy girl. Who <u>d</u>o you <u>t</u>hink <u>I</u> <u>a</u>m.

ALICE: I swear I . . . I swear I never . . .

DR. ZENO: Oh, <u>s</u>hut <u>u</u>p. <u>D</u>o <u>I</u> look <u>l</u>ike <u>a</u> polic<u>em</u>an?

ALICE: Why you take-down everything you saw me do. How I know you person not policeman. Show me what you wrote about me. [*DR. ZENO opens his notebook, shows her*] What that? Not English. [*to TERRY and VITO*] Look-like Chinese. I can't read that. Understand zer<u>o</u>.

DR. ZENO: <u>I</u> <u>c</u>an. <u>T</u>hese a<u>r</u>e <u>t</u>he <u>symbols</u> <u>I</u> <u>u</u>se. [*Reads, takes one gesture*] CCC.

ALICE: CCC.

VITO: High. He not cop. Man gentle. Fancy clothes. Look-at shoes narrow shiny.

DR. ZENO: [*to Vito*] <u>H</u>ow a<u>r</u>e <u>all</u> you<u>r</u> <u>friends</u> <u>up</u> <u>in</u> <u>N</u>ew <u>Y</u>ork?

VITO: Who told you I come-from New-York.

DR. ZENO: <u>N</u>o <u>m</u>atter. You a<u>r</u>e <u>a</u> <u>N</u>ew <u>Y</u>orke<u>r</u>. [*to ALICE*] <u>H</u>ow <u>d</u>o you <u>c</u>ome to <u>b</u>e <u>s</u>o <u>f</u>ar <u>e</u>ast? You a<u>r</u>e <u>f</u>rom <u>C</u>hicago.

ALICE: Nothing wrong move here. I have-to work.

DR. ZENO: <u>L</u>ive <u>w</u>here you <u>l</u>ike.

DR. YLVISAKER: [*to ALICE*] Calm, calm. He can't touch you; you have <u>a</u> right <u>to</u> live where you please.

ALICE: I good girl, I person.

MISS McCAIN: [*to DR. ZENO*] <u>D</u>o you know where <u>I</u> come from?

DR ZENO: <u>T</u>he <u>S</u>outh. <u>Georgia</u>.

VITO: CCC. You know everything. Really can-do (9). How?

MISS McCAIN: [*Indicates DR. YLVISAKER*] Tell him where he comes from.

DR. ZENO: <u>D</u>ifferent <u>pl</u>ace<u>s</u>. <u>I</u>t <u>i</u>s <u>h</u>ard to <u>pl</u>ace <u>h</u>im. <u>H</u>e <u>w</u>as <u>p</u>robabl<u>y</u> <u>b</u>or<u>n</u> <u>in</u> <u>C</u>onnecticut, <u>b</u>ut grew-<u>d</u> <u>up</u> <u>in</u> <u>W</u>yomin<u>g</u>.

DR. YLVISAKER: Right.

VITO: Smart. Can-do (9).

TERRY: How/how.

16

ALICE: CCC. WOW. [*to Dr. Zeno*] You deaf?

DR. ZENO: [*Hesitates*] Y . . . yes . . .

DR. YLVISAKER: May I ask you how . . .

ALICE: Don't ask. He not man gentle. He not. Always bother girls.

DR. YLVISAKER: Excuse me but I <u>would</u> like <u>to</u> ask. [*to DR. ZENO*] How <u>do</u> you <u>do</u> <u>it</u>.?

DR. ZENO: Simple <u>linguistics</u>. <u>The</u> <u>s</u>cience <u>o</u>f <u>s</u>ign <u>l</u>anguage. <u>T</u>hat <u>i</u>s my <u>p</u>rofes<u>s</u>ion. <u>A</u>lso, my <u>hobby</u>. <u>I</u> love to <u>p</u>lace <u>a</u> <u>p</u>erson . . .

ALICE: Should be-ashamed-of himself. Study people not nice.

DR. YLVISAKER: <u>Do</u> you earn your living that way?

DR. ZENO: <u>Oh</u>, yes. <u>Really</u> <u>a</u> <u>f</u>at <u>living</u>, to<u>o</u>.

ALICE: Fat living? Never heard. WELL, your business. Understand must leave girl alone.

DR. ZENO: <u>A</u> woman. <u>S</u>top <u>t</u>his <u>s</u>illy <u>t</u>alk. <u>G</u>o <u>s</u>ome<u>w</u>here.

ALICE: I have right stay here. <u>If</u> I like, stay here. Same you.

DR. ZENO: <u>A</u> woman <u>w</u>ho <u>k</u>eeps <u>s</u>igning <u>i</u>n <u>such</u> <u>a</u> <u>d</u>epres<u>s</u>ing and <u>d</u>isgu<u>st</u>ing <u>manner</u> <u>has</u> <u>no</u> right <u>to</u> <u>b</u>e <u>a</u>ny<u>w</u>here <u>no</u> right to <u>l</u>ive. <u>R</u>emember <u>t</u>hat you ar<u>e</u> <u>a</u> <u>human</u> <u>being</u> <u>w</u>ith <u>a</u> soul and <u>t</u>he <u>divine</u> gift <u>o</u>f <u>s</u>ign; <u>t</u>hat your <u>native</u> language <u>i</u>s <u>t</u>he language <u>o</u>f <u>E</u>nglish; and <u>d</u>on't stand <u>t</u>her<u>e</u> <u>gesticulating</u> . . .

VITO: <u>Ge</u> <u>st</u> <u>ic</u> . . . Spell?

DR ZENO: <u>Gesticulating</u> gesticulat<u>i</u>ng <u>l</u>ike <u>a</u> <u>s</u>ick <u>ape</u>.

VITO: [*to ALICE*] I think he mean insult you like ape.

ALICE: Not nice insult. CCC.

DR. ZENO: CCC. <u>W</u>hat <u>d</u>o you <u>m</u>ean?

ALICE: You not understand. CCC mean . . .

DR. ZENO: Nothing. It is not English. You have to make a sentence. You could have said, "Oh, no, I am not like a sick ape" and you answered "CCC"

ALICE: CCC mean . . . surprise . . . shock . . . hurt . . . etc. [throws both hands]

DR ZENO: What is that? [*Imitates "etc."*] Awful. You made up your own signs.

ALICE: ETC mean etc.

DR. ZENO: Why don't you spell it out. You could have spelled etcetera.

ALICE: Spell big+word/big+word. For for. Think high. Etce___ for high people. My sign better easy understand.

DR. ZENO: Look at her. The way she signs "CCC" and "etc". . . She should be taken out and punished for the murder of the English language.

ALICE: Sick you.

DR. ZENO: Sick you. What a sign! This is an example of an elementary education.

DR YLVISAKER: I think you picked a poor example.

DR. ZENO: Really? Look at the signs out in the street. They are dropping affixes such as ed, s, ment, etcetra . . . [*to ALICE*] ETC, everywhere. They sign any way they like. [*to VITO*] You, sir, did you go to school?

VITO: School?

DR. ZENO: School.

VITO: School. Why sign school. School. Why ask me? Think me stupid.

DR. ZENO: See, he dropped "do" and "you" in "Why ask me."

[*MISS MAUGHAN, a convention interpreter, CHAIRMAN and CONVENTION SECRETARY enter upleft and walk down the stairs.*]

Ah, there comes Miss Maughan.

18

MISS MAUGHAN: (*S.C.*) Don't start anything. Oh, no, don't. For goodness's sake.

DR. ZENO: <u>No</u>, <u>I</u> won't.

[*CONVENTION SECRETARY gives paychecks to ALICE, VITO and TERRY. Then CHAIRMAN takes MISS MAUGHAN by the arm, but DR. ZENO stops her.*]

<u>I</u> <u>would</u> like to <u>i</u>ntroduce you to <u>t</u>he <u>no</u> Engl<u>i</u>sh <u>p</u>eople. [*Points at ALICE, VITO and TERRY*]

MISS MAUGHAN: (*S.C.*) There you go again.

CHAIRMAN: "Miss Maughan, let's move on"

MISS MAUGHAN: (*S.C.*) Excuse me, <u>Dr</u>. <u>Zeno</u>. I better go. [*to USHERS*] Don't <u>pay</u> attention to <u>him</u>.

[*MISS MAUGHAN, CHAIRMAN and CONVENTION SECRETARY exit downright*]

ALICE: [*to TERRY*] Woman mad.

TERRY: She right.

DR ZENO: <u>I</u> <u>would</u> <u>r</u>ather <u>l</u>ook <u>at</u> <u>an</u> <u>i</u>nterpre<u>t</u>er <u>w</u>ith <u>p</u>roper Engl<u>i</u>sh. <u>A</u>pes gesticulate <u>i</u>n <u>a</u> <u>cage</u> [*Points at ALICE*] <u>j</u>ust <u>l</u>ike <u>t</u>his one.

ALICE: YESYESYESYES

DR ZENO: <u>What</u> <u>is</u> <u>t</u>hat? <u>I</u> ask you. You just sign "CCC" and "Sick you" and now "YESYESYESYES". <u>No</u> <u>wo</u>nder <u>s</u>he <u>can't</u> <u>r</u>ise <u>f</u>rom her <u>p</u>lace. <u>Why</u> <u>can't</u> <u>t</u>he <u>d</u>eaf <u>l</u>earn <u>h</u>ow to <u>s</u>ign Engl<u>i</u>sh. <u>Why</u> <u>can't</u> <u>t</u>he <u>d</u>eaf? You <u>s</u>ee <u>t</u>his <u>c</u>rea<u>t</u>ure <u>w</u>ith <u>h</u>er bad Engl<u>i</u>sh <u>t</u>hat <u>w</u>ill <u>k</u>eep <u>h</u>er o<u>ff</u> <u>i</u>n <u>t</u>he dark <u>wo</u>rld. <u>We</u>ll, <u>s</u>ir, <u>i</u>n six <u>month</u>s <u>I</u> <u>c</u>ould <u>p</u>ass <u>h</u>er o<u>ff</u> <u>a</u>s <u>a</u> lady at <u>a</u> <u>convention</u> ball. <u>I</u> <u>c</u>ould <u>e</u>ven get <u>h</u>er <u>a</u> <u>p</u>lace <u>a</u>s <u>a</u> <u>t</u>ea<u>c</u>her <u>o</u>r <u>s</u>ecre<u>t</u>ary, <u>w</u>hich <u>r</u>equire<u>s</u> <u>p</u>erfect Engl<u>i</u>sh.

ALICE: What that you just say before.

DR ZENO: <u>I</u> say <u>I</u> <u>c</u>oul<u>d</u> <u>p</u>ass you o<u>ff</u> <u>a</u>s <u>t</u>he <u>F</u>irst <u>L</u>ady.

ALICE: CCC [*to DR. YLVISAKER*] You believe?

DR. YLVISAKER: WELL, anything <u>is</u> possible. I myself <u>am</u> <u>a</u> student <u>of</u> the North American Indian Sign . . .

DR. ZENO: <u>Are</u> you? <u>Do</u> you <u>k</u>now <u>Dr</u>. <u>Ylvisaker</u>, <u>t</u>he <u>author</u> <u>of</u> <u>N</u>orth American <u>I</u>ndian <u>Sign</u> <u>L</u>anguage?

DR. YLVISAKER: <u>I</u> <u>am</u> <u>Dr</u>. <u>Ylvisaker</u>. Who <u>are</u> you?

DR. ZENO: <u>I</u> <u>am</u> <u>Dr</u>. <u>Zeno</u>, <u>author</u> <u>of</u> <u>USE</u>. "<u>Using</u> <u>Signed</u> <u>English</u>"

ALICE: [*to VITO*] Both famous?

VITO: I don't-know.

DR. YLVISAKER: I came from <u>t</u>he <u>W</u>est <u>t</u>o meet you!

DR. ZENO: <u>I</u> <u>was</u> <u>g</u>oing <u>t</u>o <u>t</u>he <u>W</u>est to meet you!

DR. YLVISAKER: <u>Dr</u>. <u>Zeno</u>!

DR. ZENO: <u>Dr</u>. <u>Ylvisaker</u>! [*Shake hands*] <u>W</u>here <u>are</u> you <u>staying</u>?

DR. YLVISAKER: Here in <u>t</u>his <u>h</u>otel.

ALICE: Yes. He asked me go to his room. Imagine that.

DR. YLVISAKER: I didn't.

DR. ZENO: [*to ALICE*] <u>Be</u> quiet. [*to DR. YLVISAKER*] You <u>are</u> <u>n</u>ot <u>staying</u> <u>h</u>ere. You <u>are</u> <u>staying</u> <u>at</u> my <u>p</u>lace. <u>Let</u> <u>us</u> <u>have</u> <u>drinks</u>. <u>We</u> <u>will</u> <u>have</u> <u>a</u> <u>t</u>alk.

DR YLVISAKER: Fine. I will go.

DR. ZENO: <u>N</u>orth <u>A</u>merican <u>I</u>ndian <u>Sign</u> <u>L</u>anguage <u>has</u> <u>always</u> <u>f</u>ascinate<u>d</u> me. <u>I</u> <u>have</u> <u>records</u> <u>of</u> about five.

[*MAID re-enters, walks across the lobby and exits upright.*]

DR. YLVISAKER: Have you? <u>Did</u> you know <u>there</u> <u>are</u> over 20?

DR. ZENO: My <u>G</u>od, <u>it</u> <u>is</u> <u>worse</u> <u>than</u> <u>our</u> <u>Sign</u>. <u>Do</u> you <u>k</u>now <u>them</u> <u>all</u>?

[*BOTH exit to the cocktail lounge, left.*]

ALICE: CCC. <u>U</u>.<u>S</u>.<u>E</u>. I never heard. I know Indian sign. Saw movies Indian sign.

TERRY: [*Imitating Indian*] Plain . . . see . . . buffalo . . . you . . . horse-ride . . . arrow. [*Folding arms*]

ALICE: You right. Good act. Funny you [*Pause*] <u>C</u>huck <u>C</u>huck Where [Sits on the couch] U.<u>S</u>.<u>E</u>. What that?

VITO: [*Crosses to ALICE, sits on the chair*] U.<u>S</u>.<u>E</u>. You know . . . just talked <u>at</u> convention. . . .

ALICE: <u>Busy</u> I worked . . . missed talk.

VITO: New invention . . . strange . . . different signs . . . not same ours. I not interested . . . U.<u>S</u>.<u>E</u>. for hearings . . . teachers who can't understand our Sign have-to use new signs. I watched new signs I understand zero. Mine better.

[*MARK re-enters from the hotel front downstage right.*]

ALICE: [*Sees MARK*] Why you come here?

MARK: I want tell I sorry. I not mean humiliate you. I hurry. Should be-careful.

ALICE: Your mother cold . . . not <u>care</u>.

MARK: Not her fault. My fault. I gave you trouble.

ALICE: For/for ran-away . . . left me . . . for/for.

MARK: Wait . . . let me explain.

ALICE: Sorry/sorry. [*MARK waves at her to get her attention*] Sorry. Won't forgive.

MARK: Look-at-me. I say sorry. Don't be-stubborn. I came here tell you my apologies.

VITO: [*to ALICE*] He real meant.

ALICE: I curious why you here meeting.

MARK: For demonstration.

TERRY: Show what?

VITO: Show what Deaf can do.

21

ALICE: What show?

MARK: Yes, speech . . . no, not really speech. New idea . . . called <u>Cued</u> Speech.

TERRY: <u>Cued</u>?

VITO: Never heard. Maybe belong Hearings.

ALICE: Tell me what that.

MARK: <u>Cued</u> Speech . . . for example, my name <u>is</u> <u>MARK</u>. [*Demonstrates*] MynameisMark.

ALICE: What!

TERRY: What!

VITO: What!

MARK: MynameisMark, I am <u>an</u> excellent example <u>of</u> <u>Cued</u> Speech.

VITO: You see that?

TERRY: I saw it but I don't believe it.

ALICE: You like new Speech?

MARK: No. I don't like it. I just showed how I can use <u>Cued</u> Speech because I can. You understand. With group speech, I go-on but inside I love Sign like yours.

ALICE: Why not forget.

MARK: I can't. Two more demonstrations. Then I will quit. Not really interested. I real deaf. Tell truth.

ALICE: Oh (*Y*).

MARK: You don't believe me.

ALICE: How I know. No proof. You different. Not real Deaf. You oralist.

MARK: [*Angers*] <u>No</u>. I I I Deaf like you. Can-do (*9*) talk same deaf. I happen in different <u>world</u>.

22

ALICE: Different world. Stay-out. You not belong us. Not you.

MARK: Ok. I will see you again/again. I hope when I meet you again I talk-sign, you will mind-shocked. Don't forget that. And, also, I came here to apologize you. [*He walks off downright.*]

TERRY: Don't forget that.

ALICE: Shut-up.

VITO: Handsome. Now you stuck.

ALICE: Shut-up.

[*DEAF MAN DELEGATE and DEAF MAN re-enter from the cocktail lounge left, walk across the lobby and exit downright.*]

VITO: Man deaf?

TERRY: Obvious. Look men sign.

[*CHUCK and PETE, friends of ALICE enter from the hotel front, downstage.*]

ALICE: [*Rises*] Finally. You where. Why not pick up me on time. [*CHUCK does not pay attention, ALICE taps his shoulder*] I waited/waited. Not nice. Almost in trouble.

PETE: Why?

ALICE: Man suspected me. I innocent. Man talked later insulted me. I nervous. Why not meet me on time.

PETE: What time?

ALICE: Four-o'clock.

CHUCK: Sorry. I forgot. I not interested meet people intellectual. Same they not interested us.

ALICE: Not have-to meet people. You come meet me/me. Then take me home. You stupid. [*Her hand hits his head.*]

CHUCK: Stop. Argue/argue, I bored. Now come=come. Wait. How you met man?

23

PETE: How/how?

CHUCK: Come. Tell me. How . . . where you met him.
[*Holds ALICE's wrist.*]

ALICE: Leave/leave. <u>Hurt</u>. CCC.

CHUCK: Tell-me. Tell-me.

ALICE: Ask-them [*Points at VITO and TERRY.*] Proof. They saw.

PETE: Prove! Prove!

TERRY: Yes. I saw.

VITO: True/true.

ALICE: Man happened meet me. . . here. [*CHUCK still holds her wrist.*]

CHUCK: You planned. You can (9) flirt, get man. You whore.

ALICE: [*Slaps his face, her wrist is released.*] <u>Dare</u> call me whore. I not your woman . . . not under you. Sorry you always frustrated because you fail . . . can't have me. [*VITO and TERRY laugh.*]

PETE: She mad. [*Points at ALICE.*]

CHUCK: [*to TERRY and VITO*] Finish. Enough. [*to ALICE*] Tell-me.

ALICE: I will tell you if you nice to me. Rough to me, I won't tell you. Nice, maybe I will tell.

CHUCK: [*Changes his attitude.*] Yes, now you see me man gentle. [*Sits on the couch.*] May I know how you met man.

ALICE: That better. [*Pause*] I walked out . . . happened bump man. Man young in-hurry.

PETE: Man who?

ALICE: I don't-know. Man hurry, bump-me. I fell. He ran-away. Another man helped me.

PETE: Another? Man who?

24

ALICE: I don't-know. I got-up . . . said thank-you. Man sweet, about 40. Short talk. Later Man walked-away. He deaf, look like hearing. [*Points at VITO*] He warned me Cop looked-at-me. I real . . .

PETE: Cop who? Where cop?

ALICE: I don't-know. He gone. Let me finish talk. I real innocent. That man wrote-down in book about Sign.

PETE: That man third?

ALICE: Yes.

CHUCK: Sign again. Why go to meeting? What good? Meeting/meeting about Deaf/Deaf. Always Deaf. Hearings talk/talk help Deaf. Never understand Deaf. Why not me. I know Deaf. Think Hearings smart . . .

PETE: [*Points at ALICE*] Same smart.

CHUCK: Quiet! Think Hearings smart, know alot about Deaf. No! Really same old story. Talk/talk help Deaf, not succeed.

ALICE: I know. Not worth. But want me tell you another funny happen.

PETE: Want. What/what?

CHUCK: Not about meeting.

ALICE: No. That man who bumped me, young . . . good looking. Real funny. That man said sorry. Woman . . . his mother, I think, looked cold . . . sign different.

PETE: Mother who?

ALICE: Wait! [*to CHUCK*] You know new sign, not Deaf . . . their hearings. Mother signed . . . watch me I copy . . . "Hurry, do you want me . . . miss my appo . . . Strange. I not understand.

PETE: [*to CHUCK*] She not understand.

VITO: That U.S.E.

CHUCK: U.S.E.?

PETE: I know mean use.

VITO: No. [*to CHUCK*] You not go meeting, your fault. Know/know . . . new invention. Now must sentence/sentence . . . different sign.

ALICE: Yes. Anyway that man young, good-looking. Funny. He changed/changed. To Mother sign different. To me, deaf sign.

CHUCK: I not interested. Don't see that man . . . man.

PETE: That man with book wrote-down Sign. Remember you?

CHUCK: Yes. Don't see that man again. Copy/copy Deaf Sign . . . later destroy . . . invent new sign . . . then destroy . . .

PETE: [*Jumps*] Heard/heard future deaf no-more true/true I heard.

CHUCK: Quiet!

ALICE: You misunderstand. Not that man. I talked about another man . . .

PETE: Fourth man?

ALICE: No! Man young, good-looking . . . that one who bumped me. Anyway I really mad at-him. He came-back . . .

PETE: That man fourth?

ALICE: No! No! He came back . . . said sorry to me. I still won't forgive. He signed/signed. I still stubborn, I looked-at-him . . . really good-looking, fancy clothes. I felt awful because my dress plain.

PETE: She felt awful.

ALICE: But I just looked-at . . . said nothing. He angry. He said he would see me again, then left.

CHUCK: Another man. Ok. Stay away from him, too.

ALICE: You jealous. Really nothing . . . I just talked about him. I curious where he lives. Man nice. CCC.

CHUCK: Enough. No more about man. Man. Another man.

PETE: Man fourth?

CHUCK: No matter which!

PETE: Which?

TERRY: Man nice.

VITO: Man young.

PETE: Man good-looking.

THREE: She said.

TERRY: Man stupid.

VITO: Man bad influence.

PETE: Stay <u>away</u> from him.

THREE: He said.

TERRY: Mother cold,
Signed different,
She said.

PETE: Stay <u>away</u> from him,
He said.

VITO: Man young changed/changed Signed-English to Mother Deaf-Sign to <u>Alice</u>
She said.

PETE: Stay <u>away</u> from him,
He said.

CHUCK: Shut-up.

ALICE: Shut-up.

TERRY:
VITO: Shut-up.

PETE: Both said.

TERRY: What will happen to her?

VITO: Where will she go?

PETE: Both said.

TERRY:
VITO: Shut-up.

ALICE:
CHUCK: Shut-up!

CHUCK: Get-out.

PETE: Not-know. You told me . . .

CHUCK: Get-out! All out.

[*TERRY, VITO and PETE exit downright.*]

CHUCK: [*to ALICE*] Listen, don't go to any man. Stay <u>away</u> from him. He not belong to us. You not belong to him anyway. [*Exits downright.*]

ALICE: [*Alone.*] Where I go? Who I belong? Who I am. No place. Never find right place . . . right people. People never understand me. I must force myself understand them.

BLACKOUT

ACT I: SCENE 2

SCENE:
The contemporary living room of DR. ZENO's residence. The following morning. The furniture is arranged symmetrically. Black leather couch on the center with a coffee table is between two black leather easy chairs, left and right. Near the downright wall is a bar with two high stools. A small round table is at the left wall. There is a desk with a telephone and a chair at center left. The left center opening leads to the front door (not visible). The right center opening leads to DR. ZENO's study and bedroom (not visible). Upstage is a stairway; upleft leads to the kitchen, and upright to the housekeeper's room.

OPENING, ON THE STAGE:
DR. YLVISAKER is seated on the right black chair, taking a nap. Doorbell rings. MRS. PARHAM, housekeeper for DR. ZENO, enters from the kitchen, descends the stairs, exits center left. DR ZENO enters from the study, walks to DR YLVISAKER. He taps his shoulder.

DR. YLVISAKER: [*Wakes*] <u>No</u> <u>no</u>. Let us stop. I <u>am</u> tired.

DR. ZENO: Wait. <u>Here</u> <u>is</u> <u>some</u> <u>very</u> <u>exciting</u> <u>research</u>.

DR. YLVISAKER: I have been watching <u>TV</u> all-morning. Five hours since we came here. [*Looks at wristwatch.*] Eleven-thirty.

[*MRS. PARHAM walks in from Left, waving at DR. ZENO.*]

MRS. PARHAM: (*S.C.*) <u>Are</u> you still at work? [*No answer*] <u>Excuse</u> me.

DR. ZENO: Good <u>morning</u>. <u>What</u> <u>is</u> <u>it</u>?

MRS. PARHAM: (*S.C.*) <u>A</u> young woman <u>wants</u> to see you. <u>A</u> deaf young woman.

DR. ZENO: <u>A</u> <u>deaf</u> woman! <u>What</u> <u>does</u> <u>she</u> <u>want</u>? <u>Has</u> <u>she</u> <u>an</u> <u>interesting</u> <u>way</u> <u>of</u> <u>signing</u>?

MRS. PARHAM: (*S.C.*) Yes. But I <u>don't</u> want <u>her</u> here. <u>She</u> <u>signs</u> <u>strangely</u>.

DR. ZENO: That <u>is</u> what <u>I</u> <u>want</u>. <u>Interesting</u> and <u>strange</u>. <u>Let</u> <u>her</u> <u>in</u>.

MRS. PARHAM: <u>All</u> <u>right</u>. <u>It</u> <u>is</u> you who <u>wants</u> <u>her</u> [*Returns to the front door*]

29

DR. YLVISAKER: [*Rises*] Who . . .

DR. ZENO: I will show you how I make tapes. We will set her signing. There are two TV cameras hidden in my room. [Points at the study] Don't let her look at the cameras. I want her to sign naturally. If she is aware of them, she would be nervous and her signing would look unnatural on TV.

DR. YLVISAKER: I don't know whether you are studying signing or young ladies.

[*MRS. PARHAM leads ALICE into the room.*]

MRS. PARHAM: (*S.C.*) This is the young woman.

DR. ZENO: [*Walks to her excitedly, stops and recognizes ALICE*] Why, this is the same girl I studied yesterday. I have many TV tapes of signing like hers. I am not going to waste another tape on it. Be off with you. I don't need you.

ALICE: Don't bold. You late heard why I came here for. [*to MRS. PARHAM*] Have you told him why?

MRS. PARHAM: (*S.C.*) Slow slow.

ALICE: Have . . . you . . . told . . . him . . . why?

MRS. PARHAM: He is not interested in who is coming here. [*Exits to the kitchen*]

ALICE: Please. I came here . . . because . . . I need help . . . not ask for money . . . need study . . . lessons . . . learn more . . . I will pay. I tired people made fun of me. I sick . . .

DR. ZENO: [*Sits on chair, right*] What do you want me to do for you?

ALICE: Use. I mean U.S.E. New sign same yours. Will improve my sign. I heard different sign . . . have English in Sign. I often sign to Hearings but they not understand me.

DR. ZENO: Impossible. I won't waste my time teaching you. I am not a teacher. I am interested only in research.

DR. YLVISAKER: [*to ALICE*] What <u>do</u> you want?

ALICE: I want become lady same your wife. [*to DR. ZENO*] Your wife? [Points toward the kitchen] Who? I copy her. "<u>T</u>his is <u>t</u>he young woman. <u>H</u>e <u>is</u> not intereste<u>d</u> who <u>is</u> com<u>i</u>ng here. Right me? Sign English. Right?

DR. ZENO: Right me? Sign English Right? <u>R</u>ight! <u>I</u>t <u>is</u> <u>U</u>.<u>S</u>.<u>E</u>.

DR. YLVISAKER: [*to ALICE*] Pardon me, what <u>is</u> your name?

ALICE: First <u>Alice</u>, last <u>Babel</u>.

DR. YLVISAKER: <u>Miss</u> <u>Babel</u>, won't you sit-down?

ALICE: Thank-you. [*Sits*] What <u>is</u> your name? Mind none I ask you.

DR. YLVISAKER: <u>No</u>. My name <u>is</u> <u>Dr</u>. <u>Ylvisaker</u>.

ALICE: Nice meet you. What work? You.

DR. ZENO: What work? You. You <u>s</u>houl<u>d</u> say "What <u>is</u> you<u>r</u> <u>p</u>rofess<u>i</u>on, <u>Dr</u>. <u>Ylvisaker</u>"?

ALICE: What <u>is</u> your <u>p</u>rofess<u>i</u>on, <u>Dr</u>. <u>Ylv</u>———-

DR. ZENO: <u>Dr</u>. <u>Ylvisaker</u>.

ALICE: <u>Dr</u>. <u>Ylvisa</u>——

DR. ZENO: <u>Dr</u>. <u>Ylvisaker</u>.

ALICE: <u>Dr</u>. <u>Ylvisak</u>—— Your name sign?

DR. ZENO: <u>No</u> <u>s</u>ign! Spell <u>his</u> name. <u>No</u> <u>s</u>ign name <u>f</u>or me!

ALICE: [*to DR. YLVISAKER*] Forget what I ask you.

DR. ZENO: What <u>is</u> you<u>r</u> <u>p</u>rofess<u>i</u>on, <u>Dr</u>. <u>Ylvisaker</u>?

ALICE: Spell

DR. ZENO: <u>D</u> <u>r</u>. <u>Y</u> <u>l</u> <u>v</u> <u>i</u> <u>s</u> <u>a</u> <u>k</u> <u>e</u> <u>r</u>

ALICE: Slow slow.

DR. ZENO: <u>Dr</u>. <u>Ylvisaker</u>.

ALICE: Again/again.

[*DR. ZENO turns to the sliding door, upstage.*]

ALICE: [*to DR. YLVISAKER*] Work what?

DR. YLVISAKER: Research in <u>N</u>orth American Indian Sign Language.

ALICE: Why. Study/study Indian. Their Sign different. [*Folds arms*] Stupid. Our better. Easy understand.

DR. YLVISAKER: <u>Did</u> you know that <u>there</u> <u>are</u> over 20 different sign languages among Indians?

ALICE: 20 different! CCC Deaf have one.

DR. ZENO: Why <u>d</u>o <u>we</u> waste <u>o</u>ur <u>t</u>ime <u>w</u>ith <u>h</u>er. How <u>c</u>ould <u>s</u>he <u>l</u>earn to <u>b</u>e <u>a</u> <u>l</u>ady?

ALICE: [*Rises*] I not talk to you.

DR. ZENO: [*Corrects her*] <u>I</u> <u>a</u>m not <u>t</u>alk<u>i</u>ng to you. <u>S</u>it <u>d</u>own.

[*MRS. PARHAM enters with a tray of cokes, goes to the bar.*]

Sit down. <u>S</u>it <u>d</u>own! [*ALICE sits*] How much <u>d</u>o you propose to <u>p</u>ay me <u>f</u>or <u>t</u>he <u>l</u>essons? Ten <u>d</u>ollars <u>a</u>n hour. How much <u>d</u>o you ha<u>v</u>e? You <u>n</u>eed 4 hours <u>e</u>very <u>d</u>ay. $40.00 <u>a</u> day. $200.00 <u>a</u> week. How about <u>i</u>t? <u>No</u>, you <u>c</u>an't afford <u>i</u>t. Even one <u>l</u>esson. Even if <u>I</u> <u>a</u>m <u>w</u>ill<u>i</u>ng to cut 50% <u>o</u>ff, you still <u>c</u>an't afford <u>i</u>t.

ALICE: [*Rises*] I not have much money.

MRS. PARHAM: (*S.C.*) Don't feel bad. Sit down.

DR. ZENO: <u>S</u>it <u>d</u>own [*Holds her hands, speaks orally*] "Sit down!"

ALICE: <u>Hurt</u>! You think you my father.

DR. ZENO: If <u>I</u> <u>d</u>ecide to <u>t</u>each you, <u>I</u> <u>w</u>ill <u>b</u>e <u>w</u>orse than two <u>f</u>athers to you.

DR. YLVISAKER: I have <u>an</u> idea. Remember what you have told me yesterday, that you could turn anyone into <u>a</u> <u>high</u> <u>society</u> <u>lady</u> and send her to the <u>Ball</u>. I will say that you <u>are</u> <u>the</u>

greatest teacher alive _if_ you can make that good. I will bet you all _the_ expenses _of the_ experiment you can't _do_ _it_. And I will _even_ pay for _the_ lessons.

ALICE: Sweet/sweet. You generous. Thank-you.

DR. ZENO: Sweet/sweet. You generous. Thank-you. _I_ _will_ accept _it_! _I_ _will_ make _a_ _lady_ _out_ _of_ you.

ALICE: Lady? Me out? You misunderstand me. I want learn Sign English.

DR. ZENO: Both. You _have_ to _learn_ to _behave_ like _a_ lady. [_to MRS. PARHAM_] Take _her_ to _the_ _spare_ room _upstairs_. She _will_ _stay_ here. If _she_ _gives_ you _any_ _trouble_, you _know_ what _I_ _will_ _do_.

ALICE: I call police. I _will_! True business.

DR. YLVISAKER: Be-calm, _be_ _reasonable_.

MRS. PARHAM: (_S.C._) You must be _reasonable_. Real_ly_ you must. You forget one thing about _her_. What about _her_ _parents_?

DR. ZENO: _I_ _will_ take _care_ _of_ it.

ALICE: Parents not live here. Far _C_hicago. You know where?

MRS. PARHAM: (_S.C._) What if _she_ be married?

ALICE: Who? Me married? No, not true.

DR. ZENO: Parent_s_ _or_ _no_ parent_s_. Marrie_d_ or _not_ marrie_d_. Throw _her_ _out_.

MRS. PARHAM: (_S.C._) Stop. I won't allow _it_. [_to ALICE_] Go home.

ALICE: I . . . I no home. Bum friend sleep.

DR. ZENO: Bum friend sleep. Then stay _here_.

MRS. PARHAM: (_S.C._) I must know on what term_s_ _the_ girl _is_ to _be_ here. What _is_ to _become_ of _her_ when you _have_ finishe_d_ your teac_h_ing? You must look ahead _a_ little.

DR. ZENO: What is to become of her if I threw her out of here now. Tell me.

MRS. PARHAM: (*S.C.*) That is her business, not yours.

DR. ZENO: Then when I have done with her, she can be out of here, and then it will be her business again, so that is all right.

ALICE: You cold. You have no feeling. You not care. Always think yourself. Here! That enough. Finish fed-up. I go. [*Walks off, but DR. YLVISAKER stops her.*]

DR. ZENO: That enough. Finish fed-up. I go. [*Goes to the bar*] Stay here. Do you want some coke. [*Hands a bottle of coke to her.*]

MRS. PARHAM: (*S.C.*) No no. Use glass.

DR. ZENO: [*Ignores her*] Yes?

ALICE: How I know what inside. I finish heard many girls drink know-not drugs inside, never know, same yours.

DR. ZENO: Have faith in me. [*Drinks some*] You drink the rest. [*Offers the bottle to her.*]

ALICE: [*Pause*] This not proper give bottle to lady. No thank-you.

DR. ZENO: [*Angers*] I will offer you anything you want.

ALICE: I want nothing. [*MRS. PARHAM giver her a glass of coke*] Thank you. [*to DR. ZENO*] I person good girl? Prove I right lady?

DR. YLVISAKER: Excuse me, I have-to interfere. [*Points at MRS. PARHAM*] She is right. If this girl plans to stay here with you for six months for an experiment in teaching, she must understand thoroughly what she is doing.

DR ZENO: [*to ALICE*] You are to stay here for the next six months learning how to sign properly and beautifully like a lady. If you are good and do whatever you are told, you shall sleep in a proper bedroom. If you rebel, you will sleep in the basement downstairs at the bottom of this building.

34

At the end of six months, you shall go to the Convention Ball, dressed beautifully and riding in a Cadillac. If you refuse this offer, you will be the most ungrateful wicked girl. [*to DR. YLVISAKER.*] Now, are you satisfied? [*to MRS. PARHAM*] Could I add it more clearly?

MRS. PARHAM: [*to ALICE*] (*S.C.*) Come with me.

ALICE: [*Follows her upstairs, stops*] I forget! My suitcase! Left at Train Locker. Toothpaste, toothbrush, curlers, deodorant sprayer, pajamas, clothes . . . [*As BOTH exit upright.*]

DR. YLVISAKER: Forgive my bluntness, but I hope you know what you are doing. How can you . . .

DR. ZENO: Of course, I know what I am doing. I always know what I am doing.

DR. YLVISAKER: Have you considered that for the next six months you plan to live in the same house with this girl?

DR. ZENO: Yes, yes, of course. What is wrong with that?

DR. YLVISAKER: Well, she is an extremely attractive young woman, you know.

DR. ZENO: Is she? I hadn't noticed. No, I would not called her attractive. Not at all.

DR. YLVISAKER: You don't think that she might distract you from your research? You might start to enjoy having her around. You might even fall in love with her.

DR. ZENO: What! That is ridiculous. She is just a common little girl off the street. How could I love a girl like that? And I am completely in control of my emotions! At all times! Completely!

BLACKOUT

35

ACT I: SCENE 3

SCENE:
Same, early December. Some Christmas decorations.

OPENING, ON THE STAGE:
DR. ZENO is seated in the right black chair, reading a notebook of daily reports.
Telephone rings. MRS. PARHAM runs in from the kitchen, goes to the desk and picks
up the telephone receiver.

MRS. PARHAM: [*Speaks orally.*] "Dr. Zeno's residence . . . Yes . . . Just a
moment" [*Waves at DR. ZENO, stamps on the floor.*
DR. ZENO rises, crosses to her.] (S.C.) This is Mr. Ritz.
He wants to know when you will be able to see him.
[*Reminds him*] You were supposed to see him yesterday.

DR. ZENO: Who is he? What does he want?

MRS. PARHAM: (*S.C.*) Mr. Ritz. Your research report, "A New
Discovery in . . .

DR. ZENO: Oh, tell him I am busy. Will mail the report to him.
Where is it? You know what to do.

MRS. PARHAM: [*Restrains her temper, at phone and speaks orally*]
"Mr. Ritz . . . he regrets that he will not be able to see you.
He will be very happy to send the report to you . . . Yes, it
will be mailed today . . . Oh, I am sorry. You see he is . . .
[*Looks at DR. ZENO*] . . . in the process of teaching . . .
teaching, yes. It is one of his projects he is now working
on . . . Ha ha . . . Oh, thank you very much . . . Bye bye."
[*Hangs up phone*] My my [*DR. ZENO moves to the left
black chair, sits and reads the notebook. MRS. PARHAM
follows him, sits on the couch*] (S.C.) This is not the first
time. Dr. Davis, Mr. Harris, Mrs. Thomas have called, called,
called . . . wondering what has happened. You simply can
not go on working with the girl this way. When will it stop?

DR. ZENO: When she does it properly, of course. Is that all?

MRS. PARHAM: (*S.C.*) No, sir. The mail.

37

DR. ZENO: Pay the bills and say no to the invitations. Now, the phone, say no or not here.

MRS. PARHAM: What about Christmas cards. Your dear friends have sent Christmas cards to you.

DR. ZENO: No Christmas cards this year. I don't have much time.

MRS. PARHAM: (*S.C.*) Just one thing. There is another letter from the Wives of Linguistics Club. They still want you to lecture.

DR. ZENO: Throw it away.

MRS. PARHAM: (*S.C.*) It is the third letter they have written you. You should answer it at least.

DR. ZENO: All right. Leave it on the desk. I will do it.

[*MRS. PARHAM picks up some letters from the coffee table, rises and goes to the kitchen.*]

[*ALICE storms in, followed by DR. YLVISAKER from the study*]

ALICE: I won't. I won't. I won't. I won't.

DR. YLVISAKER: Calm-down [*Moves to the right black chair, sits*]

ALICE: I won't use stupid signs.

DR. ZENO: Show me your stupid signs.

ALICE: Not my signs. Your stupid signs. OOPS Your new signs. I know my signs. I know signs before I came.

DR. ZENO: Show me my new signs.

ALICE: [*Quickly*] I was, I were, I am, he is, he was, she was . . .

DR. ZENO: Stop! What is wrong with them.

ALICE: I have-been using signs . . . was, were, am, is, are for one month and I won't sign crazy signs. Really CCC. No more. What wrong with fingerspelling?

DR. YLVISAKER: I know it is strange but try to understand . . .

DR. ZENO: [*Rises*] Strange? <u>No</u>, <u>it</u> <u>is</u> not. <u>No</u> sympathy <u>for</u> <u>her</u>. Dri<u>ll</u>ing <u>is</u> what she <u>needs</u>. Better <u>leave</u> <u>her</u> or <u>she</u> <u>will</u> <u>be</u> <u>t</u>urn<u>ing</u> to you <u>for</u> sympathy.

DR. YLVISAKER: [*Rises*] All right, if you <u>insist</u>, but have <u>a</u> little patience with her. [*Walks off upstage, exits to the kitchen.*]

ALICE: [*Follows DR. YLVISAKER, stops and turns to DR. ZENO*] You have no heart. Black hard heart. [*Turns back to the kitchen*]

DR. ZENO: [*Stops her, takes her to the couch*] <u>C</u>ontinue you<u>r</u> <u>d</u>ri<u>ll</u>ing. [*Sits on the left chair*]

ALICE: [*Sits on the couch, folds her arms. A pause. Takes a box of of Christmas cards, reads each card. She has an idea of playing with signs*] <u>S</u>ea <u>s</u>on '<u>s</u> <u>G</u>reet <u>ing</u> <u>s</u> [*No response from DR. ZENO*] <u>C</u>hrist mass <u>B</u>less <u>ing</u> <u>s</u> [*DR. ZENO makes a disapproving face*] <u>A</u> <u>C</u>hrist mass Mess age <u>for</u> you. You like this one? [*DR. ZENO makes a gesture of "No"*] Good one. Will make you smile. <u>H</u>oly <u>d</u>ay <u>C</u>heer <u>s</u> [*DR. ZENO rises, picks up a Christmas book and gives it to ALICE, returns to the chair. ALICE looks through the pages, stops and decides to do something different. She sings orally, no voice*]

Silent night, Holy night!

All is calm, [*DR. ZENO looks up at her and she stops. He resumes reading*] All is bright

Round yon Virgin Mother and Child

Holy Infant [*DR. ZENO looks up, ALICE stops, then he resumes reading*] so tender and mild,

Sleep in heavenly peace,

Sleep in heavenly peace! [*Stops, looks at DR. ZENO*]

[*ALICE looks through the pages and stops. Another idea of playing with signs*]

39

T was the night before Christmass
When all through the house
Not a creature was stirring[1], not even a mouse
The stockings[2] were hung[3] by the chimney with care
In hope that St. Nicholas[4] soon would be there

The children were nestled all snug in their beds
While . . .

DR. ZENO: [*Corrects her*] The children were nestled.

ALICE: Finish. I said exact.

DR. ZENO: Finish. I said exact. No. You did not even spell "ly" in exactly. [*Rises*] Every night before you get into bed, I want you to repeat "Night Before Christmas" fifty times.

ALICE: Fifty times! CCC Once enough. Crazy, poem too-long.

DR. ZENO: Now, another Christmas song . . . Jingle Bells
[*Walks off to the kitchen*]

ALICE: [*Alone*] Jingle bells, jingle bells
Jingle all the way!
Oh, what fun it is to ride
In a one-horse open sleigh.

Jingle bells, jingle bells
Jingle all the way!
Oh, what fun it is to ride
In a one-horse open sleigh.

Dashing through the snow,
In a one-horse open sleigh,
Over the fields we go,
Laughing all the way . . .

---

[1] Stirring as if stirring a bowl

[2] Stockings as if investing money

[3] Hung as if hung by rope

[4] Nicholas, sign for stomach, using N

[*Pauses*] Do I have-to sign like that from-now-on? To my friends? Nobody would understand me. No no . . . No? . . . N N No. Y Y Yes. Suppose all signs like that. Begin with first letter of word. OH, that too-much . . . Much? . . . L L Less. H . . . Happy . . . S . . . Sad . . . B . . . Big . . . Small . . . T . . . Tall . . . Little . . . Thin . . . F . . . Fat. World . . . People all-over should sign like that from-now-on. Live . . . Die. [*Mime*] Eat . . . [*Mime*] Work . . . [*Mime*] Play . . . [*Mime*] Sleep . . . [*Mime*] Speak . . . [*Mime*] Write . . . Read . . . Sign. They will hear . . . No, listen . . . no, see . . . they will see sign . . . Sign? . . . No? Sign.

What is the sign for . . . flowers?
Flowers . . . Birds . . . Fish . . . Animals?

What is the sign for . . . love?
Love . . . Hate
Beautiful . . . Ugly

What is the sign for . . . deaf?
Deaf . . . Deaf! . . . Deaf, my God!
Deaf and Hearing=Hearing

Deaf has only four senses.
See . . . Smell . . . Touch . . . Taste

Food! Food
Some taste bitter
Some taste sweet
Bitter . . . Sweet
Bitter, sweet

[*DR. ZENO enters, descends the stairs*]

Bitter bitter
Sweet sweet
Bitter sweet [*Bumps DR. ZENO*]

[*Pauses*] Sweet . . . sweet . . . sweet you let me come.

DR. ZENO: Stop. "Sweet you let me come" [*Corrects her*] How kind of you to let me come.

ALICE: How kind of you to let me come.

DR. ZENO: I have an idea. You will do another exercise. [*ALICE does calisthenics*] No no [*Stops her*] Now, go upstairs. [*BOTH go up and turn to the front*] Walk down gracefully. When you reach the bottom, wait for a few seconds and then say it. [*Goes to the left chair*]

ALICE: [*Talks to herself*] Tired. Feel like in-bed. Back-and-forth every/every same/same polite, always perfect sentence . . . for for. [*ALICE reaches at top*] I am . . . [*DR YLVISAKER enters, goes to the right chair*] I am . . . [*MRS. PARHAM enters, goes to the front door*] I I a am ready.

DR ZENO: Yes, I am waiting [*to DR. YLVISAKER*] She is doing some exercise. It will be beautiful.

ALICE: Good evening, Dr. . . . .Mrs. Zeno [*Descends gracefully, stops at the bottom, looks quickly at DR. YLVISAKER, runs to him*] Nice you let me come!

DR. ZENO: No no no.

ALICE: [*Corrects him*] No No.

DR. ZENO: No No.

ALICE: I know I know. How kind of you to let me come.

DR. YLVISAKER: [*to DR. ZENO*] Control yourself. Just a thought. What is wrong with it. "Nice you let me come," "Sweet you let me come."

DR. ZENO: No! It is not English. English. English. Everyone is speaking English. So sign English.

ALICE: [*Speaks orally*] "Englisssh Englisssh"

DR. YLVISAKER: Indians speak their language. So do Blacks. The Deaf, too, don't they?

DR. ZENO: I know I know. But anyone who comes here must speak English. I mean must sign English.

42

ALICE: [*Speaks orally*] "Englisssh"

DR . YLVISAKER: This is your philosophy. What about hers?

ALICE: [*Speaks orally*] "ffiloosofffyee"

DR. ZENO: She came here wishing to be taught to be a lady.

ALICE: [*Speaks orally*] Laadiiee" [*Signs big*] How kind of you to let me come.

[*MRS. PARHAM enters with several Christmas parcels*]

MRS. PARHAM: (*S.C.*) Here is your Christmas mail.

ALICE: [*to DR. ZENO*] How kind of you to let me come.

[*DR. ZENO takes the mail from MRS. PARHAM, marches off to the study.*]

MRS. PARHAM: "Dr. Zeno . . . Dr. Zeno . . . "

ALICE: [*to DR. YLVISAKER*] How kind of you to let me come.

[*DR. YLVISAKER walks off to the study*]

MRS. PARHAM: "My my"

ALICE: [*to MRS. PARHAM*] How kind of you to let me come.

MRS. PARHAM: (*S.C.*) Pardon me. What did you say?

ALICE: [*Excited*] How kind of you to let me come.

MRS. PARHAM: (*S.C.*) Me? I did not ask you to come. Dr. Zeno did. [*Goes up, mumbling to herself and exits to the kitchen.*]

ALICE: [*Speaks orally to herself*] "Englisssh Englisssh ffiloosoffyee laadiiee Englisssh" [*Stops, facing audience*] How kind of you to let me come! [*Bows gracefully*]

BLACKOUT

ACT I: SCENE 4

SCENE:
Same, late March at midnight.

OPENING, ON THE STAGE:
DR. YLVISAKER in bathrobe lies on the couch. DR. ZENO in bathrobe, sits in the right chair, reading a notebook. MRS. PARHAM brings a tray with a glass of milk, cookies and several cans of beer, places it on the bar. ALICE in a lounge robe runs in, stops and walks quietly to the left chair. Something is strange, she looks pregnant. She sits calmly. MRS. PARHAM offers her the glass of milk and the cookies.

DR. ZENO: <u>No no</u>. <u>D</u>on't give <u>her</u>.

[MRS. PARHAM returns the glass to the bar and waves at everyone.]

MRS. PARHAM: "Good night. Good night. Good night, Alice"
[Exits to her bedroom upright]

DR. ZENO: *[Suspicious, waves at ALICE]* Get-up. You. <u>P</u>lease get <u>up</u>.

[ALICE puts her hands on her tummy, rises slowly.]

ALICE: *[Speaks orally]* "Why?"

DR. ZENO: What <u>is</u> <u>t</u>he matter . . . *[Sees her hands on her tummy]* <u>No no no no</u> *[Looks at DR. YLVISAKER]* You you you.

DR. YLVISAKER: <u>What</u>? Me? What <u>did</u> I <u>do</u>?

DR. ZENO: *[Walks to ALICE]* What happened?

ALICE: *[Speaks orally]* "nothing"

DR. ZENO: Come here. *[ALICE does not move. He takes her hands up and about twenty comic books fall from her "tummy," scattering about the floor]* <u>Comic</u> <u>books</u>! Why? Why?

ALICE: Comic books good . . . always learn/learn.

DR. ZENO: <u>No no no comic</u> book <u>in</u> <u>t</u>his <u>p</u>lace. You <u>k</u>now what you <u>are</u> supposed to <u>do</u> . . . <u>D</u>o the "<u>Daffodils</u>". *[Returns to the chair]*

ALICE: [*Stamps on the floor*] I can't. [*Sits*] I tired. I am so tired. I tired.

DR. ZENO: I tired. I am tired!

ALICE: Headache. Bang bang. Blow-up.

DR. ZENO: You have forgotten yourself.

ALICE: Sorry. I have a head ache.

DR. ZENO: I know you are tired. I know your headaches. But think what you are trying to accomplish. Think what you are dealing with. Now we have only two weeks to go . . . remember you will use U.S.E. at the Ball. You have to show them. That is what you have set yourself to prove and you will succeed. Now, try it again.

ALICE: [*Slowly*] I wandered lonely as a cloud

DR. ZENO: Yes.

ALICE: That floats on high over vales and hills.

DR. ZENO: Again.

ALICE: I wandered lonely as [*Rises*] a cloud that floats on high over vales and hills.

DR. ZENO: [*to DR. YLVISAKER*] I think she has got it.

ALICE: When all at once I saw a crowd

DR. ZENO: Yes yes.

ALICE: A host of golden daffodils, Beside the lake, beneath the trees Fluttering and dancing in the breeze. [*DR. ZENO rises, joins her*] Continuous as the stars that shine and twinkle on the milky way. They stretched in never-ending line. [*DR. YLVISAKER rises, joins them*] Ten thousand saw I at a glance. Tossing their heads in sprightly dance. [*All THREE dance around*]

ALICE: Right?

DR. ZENO: Yes!

[*ALICE runs to him, hugs him and then to DR. YLVISAKER, hugs. She goes up the stairs, and then down slowly like a lady. DR. ZENO runs to her, holds her hand and leads her to the couch. She sits gracefully like an actress. DR. YLVISAKER offers imaginary flowers to her and she accepts with pleasure. DR. ZENO offers an imaginary glass of champagne and she takes it and drinks. She throws the "flowers" and "glass" in the air and gets up and jumps over the couch. Both men chase her up the stairway. Then she jumps down the stairs. DR. ZENO shows disapproval of her manner; she changes and both men show approval. She hugs both men. MRS. PARHAM re-enters, wearing bathrobe and looks scared and confused.*]

DR. ZENO: [*to DR. YLVISAKER*] We are making fine progress. I think the time has come to try her out.

[*ALICE quietly walks away, picks up comic books and goes to the bar and drinks milk and eats some cookies.*]

MRS. PARHAM: (*S.C.*) Are you feeling all right.

DR. ZENO:
DR. YLVISAKER: Great! Thank you. And you?

MRS. PARHAM: Fine, Thank you.

DR. ZENO: Splendid. [*to DR. YLVISAKER*] Let us test her in public and see how she fares.

MRS. PARHAM: (*S.C.*) Do you wish to see me?

DR. ZENO: Me? I did not call you.

MRS. PARHAM: (*S.C.*) It seems that you have made the noises. I had to come down. I thought maybe you want something to eat.

DR. ZENO: Dinner! [*to DR. YLVISAKER*] I know! Let us take her to the restaurant.

DR. YLVISAKER: The restaurant?

MRS. PARHAM: "Oh, no, my dear" (*S.C.*) I don't wish to go to the restaurant at this hour.

47

DR. ZENO: Not you. I will take Alice to the restaurant tomorrow.

MRS. PARHAM: Are you all right?

DR. ZENO: I will call Miss Maughan and invite her here and then we will go to the restaurant. What is the name of the place . . . it is near the park.

MRS. PARHAM: (*S.C.*) The Garden Restaurant.

DR. ZENO: Yes, that is it. We will surprise her. We will buy her a dress. [*to MRS. PARHAM*] Where do you buy a lady's gown?

MRS. PARHAM: "I beg your pardon."

DR. ZENO: Oh, no, not for you. It is for Alice.

MRS. PARHAM: (*S.C.*) At the Saks.

DR. ZENO: Thank you. [*Kisses her hand*]

MRS. PARHAM: "I beg your pardon." (*S.C.*) I don't understand what it is all about.

DR. ZENO: Alice has got it. Will you call Miss Maughan early in the morning. Tell her to come here at one o'clock tomorrow.

MRS. PARHAM: "All right." [*Checks*] (*S.C.*) Here at one o'clock. I will call tomorrow.

DR. ZENO: Right. Call her at seven in the morning. I will be off to bed. Good night. [*Goes to ALICE*] Good night.

ALICE: Good night.

[*DR. ZENO exits to his bedroom, right.*]

DR. YLVISAKER: [*to MRS. PARHAM*] Good night. [*to ALICE*] Have a good sleep tonight.

ALICE: Good night. [*Kisses him lightly*]

DR. YLVISAKER: Good night. [*Goes off to the bedroom, right*]

48

MRS. PARHAM: [*to ALICE*] (*S.C.*) You have all been working much too hard. I think the strain is beginning to show. I don't care what Dr. Zeno says, you must forget your work and go to bed. We will go out to a movie tomorrow . . . no no . . . day after tomorrow.

ALICE: Thank you. You have-been sweet to me. Good night.

MRS. PARHAM: "Good night, my girl."

[*MRS. PARHAM goes up, mumbling to herself and exits to her bedroom, upright.*]

ALICE: [*Thinks of* "The Daffodils," *walks about the room and signs in her own translation*]

The waves beside them danced, but they
Outdid the sparkling waves in glee:
A poet could not but be gay
In such jocund company.
I gazed and gazed but little thought
What wealth the show to me had brought:

For often, when on my couch I lie
In vacant or in pensive mood,
They flash upon that inward eye
Which is the bliss of solitude;
And then my heart with pleasure fills,
And dances with the daffodils.

BLACKOUT

ACT I: SCENE 5

SCENE:
Same, the following day.

OPENING, ON THE STAGE:
DR YLVISAKER and MISS MAUGHAN are seated on the couch. DR. YLVISAKER has a book of Indian Sign Language, shows it to MISS MAUGHAN who holds a glass of sherry.

DR. YLVISAKER: [*Shows her his book*] See the difference between Cheyenne and Sioux.

MISS MAUGHAN: Very interesting. Yes, it is fantastic.

DR. YLVISAKER: You think it is possible to use in your work?

MISS MAUGHAN: "Oh, no." You see, my line is different. Mine is absolutely for the deaf and yours is strictly for Indians. I don't want to mix two languages in my work.

DR. YLVISAKER: I understand but I believe there is a relation between . . .

MISS MAUGHAN: Enough. I don't wish to hear it. I have been interpreting for over 25 years and interpretation is my profession. I have known the Deaf and I am proud of it.

DR. YLVISAKER: Yes, I know you have deaf parents, teach deaf children, work with deaf adults. I am not discussing the Deaf. I am only interested in Sign.

MISS MAUGHAN: "Dr. Ylvisaker," I don't understand why you . . . no, Dr. Zeno wants me to come here today. And then go out to the Garden Restaurant.

DR. YLVISAKER: He wants to show his experiment and . . .

MISS MAUGHAN: "Oh, no, not again." Why at the Garden Restaurant?

DR. YLVISAKER: Have a little patience. He will be here shortly.

51

MISS MAUGHAN: His call really scared me. At that hour . . . "yes" . . . it was seven o'clock in the morning. Why could not he simply wait until a proper time like ten in the morning.

DR. YLVISAKER: It would be inconvenient for you anyway.

MISS MAUGHAN: What a disagreeable surprise. The Garden Restaurant is usually the one place I can go to with my friends and not risk seeing Dr. Zeno. Whenever my friends meet him, I never see my friends again.

DR. YLVISAKER: He needs you. You see, he is taking a girl to the annual Convention Ball, and he wanted to try her out first.

MISS MAUGHAN: A girl? I beg your pardon.

DR. YLVISAKER: You know . . . the annual Convention Ball.

MISS MAUGHAN: Yes, I know the Ball, but what girl?

DR. YLVISAKER: Yes. You see . . . I met him when he happened to meet Miss Babel, who now lives here.

MISS MAUGHAN: Lives with Dr. Zeno! "Oh," a love affair?

DR. YLVISAKER: No no . . . she is an usher. He happened, I say, happened to meet her.

MISS MAUGHAN: An usher . . . you mean an usher.

DR. YLVISAKER: Yes, he said to me: 'In six months I could pass her off as a lady at a convention ball.' And I said, 'Impossible' and he answered 'Yes, I can.'

[*The doorbell rings.*]

MISS MAUGHAN: [*Startled by the ring*] I still don't understand. Is he taking an usher to the Garden Restaurant with us?

DR. YLVISAKER: That is it.

[*MRS. PARHAM enters, descends and goes to the front door. DR. ZENO enters from his bedroom, walks straight to MISS MAUGHAN*]

MISS MAUGHAN: I have heard you have an usher here.

DR. ZENO: [*Turns to DR. YLVISAKER, and then to her*] She will be all right. I have taught her. You will be quite safe.

MISS MAUGHAN: Safe? Where is the girl now?

DR. ZENO: Don't worry. She will be here in a moment. Excuse me. I will be right back.

[*MRS. PARHAM guides MRS. NEWTON and MARK into the room.*]

MISS MAUGHAN: [*Rises*] "Ah, Mrs. Newton."

DR. ZENO: [*Surprised*] Are these people with you?

MISS MAUGHAN: Yes, I have a plan with them for today and today you insisted my coming here. I told them to meet here.

DR. ZENO: Damn! Damn! [*Exits upright*]

MRS. NEWTON: (*S.C.*) Is this one who has the weird experiment?

MISS MAUGHAN: "Sshh . . . not a word about him. His friend is here."
                Dr. Ylvisaker, this is Mrs. Newton. This is Dr. Ylvisaker.

MRS. NEWTON: "How do you do?"

DR. YLVISAKER: How do you do?

MISS MAUGHAN: This is her son, Mark. Dr. Ylvisaker.

MARK: Hi.

DR. YLVISAKER: Nice to meet you.

[*MARK is seated in the right chair; MRS. NEWTON on the couch right and MISS MAUGHAN on the couch left; DR. YLVISAKER in the left chair. MISS MAUGHAN and MRS. NEWTON speak orally for a while. MRS. PARHAM re-enters with a tray with sherry bottle and glasses, walks to the bar. DR. ZENO and ALICE in a special dinner dress and a white hat enter, descent the stairway. DR. YLVISAKER and MARK rise.*]

DR. ZENO: May I introduce Miss Alice Babel?

MISS MAUGHAN: "My dear Miss Babel."

ALICE: How <u>k</u>ind <u>o</u>f you to <u>l</u>et me <u>c</u>ome.

DR. ZENO: <u>No</u> <u>no</u>.

MISS MAUGHAN: Come? [*Changes*] Delighted, "my dear." [*Introduces*] <u>Mrs</u>. <u>Newton</u>. "Miss Babel."

MRS. NEWTON: "How do you do?"

ALICE: How <u>k</u>ind . . . [*Changes*] How <u>do</u> you <u>do</u>?

MISS MAUGHAN: And her son <u>Mark</u>.

ALICE: [*Recognizes him*] How . . . how <u>do</u> you <u>do</u>?

MARK: How do you do?

[*ALL sit. ALICE, nervous of MARK, tries to hide her face with the hat.*]

MARK: I believe I have met you before.

ALICE: <u>No</u>, I don't think.

MARK: I think I met you last fall . . . <u>at</u> <u>the</u> convention.

ALICE: Convention? <u>No</u>.

[*Silence. MRS. NEWTON and MISS MAUGHAN talk to each other. ALICE tries to read their lips. Then she bursts into laughter.*]

DR. ZENO: <u>No</u> <u>no</u> <u>no</u>.

MISS MAUGHAN: "Oh," on <u>the</u> way here, I heard <u>the</u> <u>radio</u> saying <u>there</u> will <u>be</u> rain this afternoon. [*Looks at the window door upstage*] <u>The</u> <u>clouds</u> <u>are</u> coming.

ALICE: I wandered lonely as a cloud that floats . . .

DR. ZENO: <u>NO</u> <u>NO</u> <u>NO</u>

ALICE: <u>At</u> <u>the</u> restaurant . . . you will see flowers . . . <u>daffodils</u> all-over. [*to MRS. NEWTON*] Flowers . . . "flooowerrr."

MRS. NEWTON: "Oh oh oh," <u>I</u> <u>do</u> <u>h</u>ope <u>the</u> <u>c</u>loud<u>s</u> <u>w</u>ill not <u>b</u>reak. <u>O</u>ur <u>f</u>amily always <u>c</u>atch <u>c</u>old.

ALICE: Same. I had colds last week. It really knock me on my back.

MRS. NEWTON: Knock on your back?

ALICE: [*Corrects her sign*] Yes. Sick . . . . . . laid me out.

MRS. NEWTON: Laid you out?

ALICE: [*Corrects her sign*] Yes, lay.

DR. ZENO: OH . . . that is the new small sign. It means sick.

MRS. NEWTON: "Oh oh oh," I am sorry. I hope you are feeling better.

ALICE: Yes, I feel better . . . strong [*Large sign*].

MRS. NEWTON: "Oh oh oh," I am glad.

ALICE: Know how? I had scotch drink . . . [*DR. ZENO alerts her, she changes*] Scotch . . . Scotch plaid blanket over-me. Warm . . . nestled.

MRS. NEWTON: "What is it?"

ALICE: [*to MISS MAUGHAN*] Tell her.

MISS MAUGHAN: "Nestled."

MRS. NEWTON: "Oh oh oh."

MARK: That sign really far-out.

MRS. NEWTON: "What is it?"

ALICE: Far-out. [*to MISS MAUGHAN*] Tell her.

MISS MAUGHAN: "Far out"

MRS. NEWTON: "Oh oh oh."

ALICE: [*to MARK*] If I sign proper, why you laugh-at-me? [*Waves at DR. ZENO*] Have I said anything wrong?

MISS MAUGHAN: Not at all, "my dear."

ALICE: WELL, I don't understand. What I want say . . .

55

DR. YLVISAKER: [*Rises*] I don't suppose there is enough time. [*to DR. ZENO*] Let us go.

[*ALL rise*]

ALICE: Yes! Let go. Wonderful! [*Bumps MRS. NEWTON down and then bumps MISS MAUGHAN down. She realizes her mistake, decides to fall down herself.*]

BLACKOUT

ACT I: SCENE 6

SCENE:
A reception room next to the Pilgrim Hotel Ballroom, two weeks later in
April. On the floor are two round tables with flowers and champagne glasses;
chandeliers above the tables. There are two candelabras on the platform upstage.
Upstage center is the main entrance; left center leads into the ballroom (not visible).
NOTE: All men wear black tie and the women evening gowns.

OPENING, ON THE STAGE:
WAITER enters from the ballroom, carrying tray of champagne glasses and
places it on the right table. CHAIRMAN follows him, checks the reception
room. CONVENTION SECRETARY walks in from the main entrance, takes a
glass of champagne and drinks. WAITER exits upstage. CHAIRMAN speaks
orally to SECRETARY. MISS McCAIN wanders in, sees CHAIRMAN and tries
to introduce herself.

MISS McCAIN: "Haalloo."

CHAIRMAN: "Good evening, Miss . . . "

MISS McCAIN: "Shkimeen."

CHAIRMAN: "Pardon me."

MISS McCAIN: "Shkiimeen."

CHAIRMAN: "I am sorry but I can't hear."

MISS McCAIN: [*Writes her name in the air, "Chimene"*] "C H I M E N E"

CHAIRMAN: "Oh oh." [*to SECRETARY*] This is Idontevenunderstandher."
[*to MISS McCAIN*] "This is Miss Essex."

SECRETARY: "How do you do?"

MISS McCAIN: "haow doo you doo?"

SECRETARY: "Yoou . . . er . . . you have aprettydre . . . gown."

MISS McCAIN: "Thaak yoou. Yoou, tooo."

[*DEAF WOMAN enters, looks helpless and moves to the left table. CHAIRMAN offers MISS McCAIN a glass of champagne and makes a gesture of "you-may-go-to-the-ballroom". She turns, sees the DEAF WOMAN and walks to her. DEAF HUSBAND and WIFE come in from the ballroom, meet the women and sign about the ballroom. WAITER runs in, whispers to SECRETARY who then excuses herself and follows WAITER to the main entrance. CHAIRMAN walks off to the ballroom. DR. YLVISAKER enters upstage, looks nervous at DR. ZENO follows him.*]

DR. YLVISAKER: If there is any mishap here tonight . . . if Alice gets embarrassed, she will walk out. I have been begging you to call-off this experiment ever since that time at the restaurant.

DR. ZENO: Alice can do anything. Miss Maughan loves her. She did beautifully at the restaurant. She won't bump anyone.

DR. YLVISAKER: But think of the trouble it might be! If anything happens tonight, I don't know what I will do.

DR. ZENO: Don't worry. You could always go back to the Indians. Have a drink. It will calm your nerves.

DR. YLVISAKER: No, I am not nervous. [*Goes to the ballroom, stops and turns back to DR. ZENO*] Give me some.

[*DR. ZENO hands him a glass of champagne. MISS McCAIN recognizes DR. YLVISAKER, goes over to him.*]

MISS McCAIN: "Haalloo" [*Offers her hand to him*]

DR. YLVISAKER: "Hello." [*Accepts her hand*]

MISS McCAIN: "Remember me?"

DR. YLVISAKER: "I am sorry . . . " [*Picks up a glass of champagne, gives it to and guides her to the group of people. Turns to DR. ZENO*] Who is she? [*DR. ZENO shrugs. Then, he reminds him*] Are you so sure she will manage by herself.

DR. ZENO: We will see.

DR. YLVISAKER: Suppose she doesn't.

DR. ZENO: Then I lose my bet.

[*MISS MAUGHAN enter upstage, walks to DR. ZENO.*]

DR. YLVISAKER: Good evening, . . .

MISS MAUGHAN: Excuse me, I heard some people asking who the lady was. Do tell me what has happened.

DR. YLVISAKER: What lady?

MISS MAUGHAN: I don't know but she just walked in the hall. She should be here. [*Looks toward the ballroom*] I do not see her.

[*MRS. NEWTON and MARK enter upstage, meet their friends.*]

DR. YLVISAKER: [*to MRS. NEWTON*] Good evening.

MRS. NEWTON: "Good evening, Dr. Ylvisaker."

DR. YLVISAKER: [*to MARK*] Good evening.

MARK: Good evening.

MRS. NEWTON: [*to MISS MAUGHAN*] "Good evening."

MISS MAUGHAN: "Good evening."

[*They gather around the table, take glasses and sip. Ad libs. BELLBOY enter, calls MISS MAUGHAN. Both exit upstage.*]

DR. YLVISAKER: [*to Dr. Zeno*] I am nervous. Where is Alice?

DR. ZENO: [*Calmly*] Upstairs. She is coming.

DR. YLVISAKER: I think I had better leave. This waiting is worse than watching her come in.

DR. ZENO: Calm down. She will be right here.

MRS. NEWTON: [*to DR. ZENO*] The First Lady is here for the Ball . . . not to meet Alice.

DR. ZENO: Alice is here for the Ball . . . to meet the First Lady!

[DEAF LADY and her escort HEARING MAN enter, meet the DEAF group. Ad libs. CHAIRMAN re-enters, tries to get the people into the ballroom. THE FIRST LADY, SECRETARY, MISS MAUGHAN and SECURITY MAN arrive upstage. CHAIRMAN goes to the FIRST LADY, escorts her down the stairs. MISS MAUGHAN goes to her left, where she will stay to interpret.]

CHAIRMAN: *[with MISS MAUGHAN]* "Ladies and gentlemen, we are deeply honored tonight to have with us the First Lady of our country."

[Slight applause from the crowd.]

FIRST LADY: *[with MISS MAUGHAN]* "My dear friends. How kind of you to ask me to come to your nice party. The President asked me to tell you that he is very sorry that he cannot be here. Actually, he is not a very good dancer anyway, *[Laughter from the crowd]* so I think we shall get along very well without him."

[Polite applause from the crowd. DR. ZENO moves to CHAIRMAN.]

CHAIRMAN: *[with MISS MAUGHAN]* "I would like to introduce to you Professor Albert Zeno, our famous expert on English and Sign Language. More than anyone else in America, he helps the deaf to communicate with the hearing. We say about him that he knows it all, from A to Z."

[FIRST LADY greets him, extends her hand. DR. ZENO, with a little bow, takes it. ALICE enters upstage, stands quietly. DR. ZENO sees her, goes to her and escorts her down the stairs. Ad libs from the crowd.]

DR. ZENO: *[with MISS MAUGHAN, to FIRST LADY]* I would like to present to you, Miss Alice Babel, one of my students.

ALICE: *[with MISS MAUGHAN]* How do you do? *[to DR. ZENO]* How kind of you to let me come. *[to EVERYONE]* How kind of you to let me come!

[Ad libs from the crowd]

DR. ZENO: Please! Don't do that!

FIRST LADY: [*with MISS MAUGHAN*] "Do all professors have such pretty students? How lucky for them!"

DR. ZENO: [*with MISS MAUGHAN*] No no. Not lucky.

ALICE: I wandered lonely as a cloud that floats on high . . .

[*Ad libs from the crowd.*]

FIRST LADY: [*to MISS MAUGHAN*] "What is she saying?"

MISS MAUGHAN: (*S.C.*) "Something about being lonely. She was lonely."

FIRST LADY: [*with MISS MAUGHAN, to ALICE*] "My dear child. How could you be lonely? No one so sweet and pretty should ever be lonely."

ALICE: [*with MISS MAUGHAN*] How kind of you to let me come! How very, very kind of you to let me come . . .

DR. ZENO: Stop! I beg you, please, please stop.

FIRST LADY: [*with MISS MAUGHAN, to DR. ZENO*] "Did you say something?"

DR. ZENO: [*with MISS MAUGHAN*] No, no. I was just saying, she should stop taking so much of your time.

FIRST LADY: [*with MISS MAUGHAN*] "Nonsense. She is a perfectly charming girl. I am sure you a very cruel teacher to her."

DR. ZENO: Who? Me?

FIRST LADY: [*to MISS MAUGHAN*] "Ask her if she will come and talk to me, later in the evening, when she has some free time."

MISS MAUGHAN: [*to ALICE, signs*] The First Lady would like you to come and talk to her later, when you are free. Will you?

ALICE: [*with MISS MAUGHAN*] OH Yes. I will be very happy to do that. How kind of you to let me come.

[*FIRST LADY, escorted by CHAIRMAN, walks off to the ballroom, followed by the people except DR. ZENO, ALICE and MARK.*]

DR. ZENO: Stop that! Please, you must stop that!

ALICE: Right act me? Perfect?

[*DR. ZENO straightens himself. ALICE turns her face to MARK who moves a few steps to her. She turns back, gets ready for the ball. DR. ZENO stands firmly; ALICE extends her hand and puts it on his hand; both walk grandiosely to the ballroom leaving MARK alone.*]

BLACKOUT

ACT II: SCENE 1

SCENE:
Pilgrim Hotel Lobby after the ball.

OPENING, ON THE STAGE:
BELLBOY behind the desk, speaks orally to MAID. DEAF HUSBAND and WIFE come in with DEAF WOMAN, left center, cross to downstage right and exit to the hotel front. MAID hurries to exit upstage right. DEAF LADY and HEARING MAN with his shoes enter; he limps and mutters to himself and LADY tries to assist him. Both exit downstage right. DR. ZENO and ALICE walk in left center, go to the upstage stairway; DR. YLVISAKER runs in, stops DR. ZENO.

DR. YLVISAKER: It <u>was</u> <u>a</u> great <u>achievement</u>.

DR. ZENO: Yes.

[*ALICE moves quietly, sits on the easy chair.*]

DR. YLVISAKER: <u>Absolutely</u> <u>fantastic</u>.

DR. ZENO: Yes.

DR. YLVISAKER: I congratulate you.

DR. ZENO: Thank you.

DR. YLVISAKER: You <u>did</u> <u>it</u>! I remember you said you <u>would</u> <u>do</u> <u>it</u>. I doubted you could <u>do</u> <u>it</u>. But now I must admit <u>it</u> <u>was</u> <u>a</u> success. You <u>deserve</u> <u>a</u> medal.

DR. ZENO: It <u>was</u> nothing, <u>really</u> nothing.

DR. YLVISAKER: You <u>did</u> <u>it</u> all <u>by</u> yourself.

DR. ZENO: <u>All</u> <u>I</u> can say <u>is</u>, thank <u>God</u> <u>it</u> <u>is</u> <u>all</u> <u>over</u>. Now <u>I</u> can go to bed <u>at</u> <u>least</u> without <u>dreading</u> tomorrow.

[*CHAIRMAN and SECRETARY enter from left center, slightly zigzagging to downstage right.*]

CHAIRMAN: [*Waves*] "Good evening."

SECRETARY: [*Tries to control him, to DR. ZENO*] "Good night."
[*to CHAIRMAN*] "Please . . . Shhh . . . let us get out . . . "

DR. YLVISAKER: Good night.

[*CHAIRMAN and SECRETARY exit to the hotel front.*]

DR. ZENO: Good night.

DR. YLVISAKER: We will go home. What time will we leave tomorrow?

DR. ZENO: [*Looks at his wristwatch*] Say, ten o'clock.

DR. YLVISAKER: Ok. I will be here in the lobby before ten. Good night.
[*to ALICE*] Good night.

DR. ZENO: Good night.

[*DR. YLVISAKER exits upright.*]

ALICE: Good . . .

DR. ZENO: [*to ALICE*] Come, go to bed. [*ALICE does not rise or move*] Are not you listening? [*No answer*] What is the matter? Is anything wrong?

ALICE: Nothing wrong with you person. [*Rises*] I finally won your bet for you. Right? That enough for you. For me person not matter to you.

DR. ZENO: You won my bet! You! I won it.

ALICE: I wish I could kill you. You selfish egoist. Why you met me here. Why not you leave me here. You thanked God it is all over . . . and you can now throw me out.

DR. ZENO: You are nervous and over-tired. [*ALICE tries to scratch his face, he mouths*] "Stop! Sit down."

ALICE: What will happen to me? [*Sits on the couch*] What will happen to me?

DR. ZENO: How the hell do I know what will happen to you? What does it matter what becomes of you?

ALICE: You not <u>care</u>. I know you not <u>care</u>. I dead, you still
not <u>care</u>.

DR. ZENO: [*Sits*] Why <u>have</u> you sudden<u>ly</u> begu<u>n</u> go<u>i</u>ng on like
<u>th</u>is? <u>May I</u> ask whether you complain about your
<u>treatment</u> here?

ALICE: No.

DR. ZENO: <u>Has</u> <u>any</u>body <u>behaved</u> bad<u>ly</u> to you?

ALICE: No.

DR. ZENO: <u>Dr</u>. <u>Ylvisaker</u>?

ALICE: No.

DR. ZENO: Me?

ALICE: [*Pauses*] No.

DR. ZENO: <u>I</u> am <u>g</u>lad to hear <u>i</u>t. <u>Pe</u>rhaps you <u>are ti</u>red after <u>t</u>he <u>ball</u>.
It <u>is</u> <u>all</u> <u>o</u>ver now. <u>The</u>re <u>is</u> nothing more to <u>w</u>orry about.

ALICE: No . . . Nothing more for you to worry about. OH God,
I wish I <u>was</u> dead. [*Turns away from him*]

DR. ZENO: [*Tries to console her*] Why? <u>L</u>isten to me.

ALICE: [*to herself*] I not understand. I ignorant. Stupid/stupid.

DR. ZENO: [*Gently holds her face*] It <u>is</u> <u>only</u> your <u>i</u>maginat<u>i</u>on.
<u>No</u>body <u>is</u> hurt<u>i</u>ng you. Nothing <u>is</u> wrong. Now you <u>are</u>
free and can <u>d</u>o what<u>e</u>ver you like.

ALICE: Where I go? What I <u>do</u>? What will happen to me.

DR. ZENO: <u>Oh</u>, <u>t</u>hat <u>is</u> what <u>is</u> bother<u>i</u>ng you, <u>is i</u>t? [*Rises*] <u>I</u> <u>did</u> not
<u>re</u>alize you we<u>re</u> go<u>i</u>ng away. You <u>might</u> <u>w</u>ork, you know.
You <u>are</u> not bad look<u>i</u>ng. You <u>have</u> <u>been</u> upset but when
you <u>are</u> <u>f</u>eel<u>i</u>ng <u>well</u> and <u>quite</u> yourself, you <u>are</u> what <u>I</u>
<u>could</u> call attract<u>i</u>ve.

ALICE: [*Rises*] I not fit go to any place.

DR. ZENO: <u>Oh</u>, come-on. <u>The</u> <u>f</u>uture <u>w</u>orrie<u>s</u> you.

ALICE: What else can I d<u>o</u>?

DR. ZENO: <u>Oh</u>, lot<u>s</u> <u>o</u>f <u>th</u>ing<u>s</u>. <u>Dr</u>. <u>Y</u>lvisaker <u>w</u>ill help you. <u>Oh</u>, come. You <u>w</u>ill <u>b</u>e <u>a</u>ll <u>r</u>ight. <u>I</u> must <u>b</u>e <u>o</u>ff to bed. <u>I</u> <u>a</u>m <u>v</u>ery sleep<u>y</u>.

ALICE: <u>Ok</u>. Now I can stand on my <u>own</u>.

DR. ZENO: <u>I</u> <u>p</u>refer to <u>s</u>ay nothing more tonight. <u>I</u> <u>a</u>m going to bed. You, to<u>o</u>.

ALICE: Good night! <u>I</u> <u>a</u>m going to bed! You, to<u>o</u>! [*Runs upstage, exits right*]

DR. ZENO: [*to himself*] <u>D</u>amn . . . <u>d</u>amn plan . . . <u>d</u>amn my <u>e</u>xper<u>im</u>ent . . . <u>d</u>amn all . . . <u>d</u>amn <u>d</u>amn <u>d</u>amn [*as he exits upstage right*]

[*MISS McCAIN walks in from the ballroom, goes to the hotel front, exits. BELLBOY enters, goes to the desk. MAID and JANITOR come in from upstage left, talk with the BELLBOY. MISS McCAIN re-enters, looks concerned, runs to the couch and sits. PETE follows, walks to her.*]

PETE: Matter/matter?

MISS McCAIN: I say <u>No</u>.

PETE: Please. Nothing take you out.

MISS McCAIN: <u>No</u> . . . not with you. Why you always bother me. I don't-want mix with deaf. Always trouble. Hearings better, never trouble.

PETE: Compare/compare. Really no difference.

MISS McCAIN: Deaf always spread ruin names. I don't-like.

PETE: Hearings same. Behind you they call-you-names and you know-nothing.

MISS McCAIN: Why you came here . . . curious what we <u>do</u>=<u>do</u>. You not invited . . . big-head you invaded. I not interested talk with you.

PETE: Ok . . . no talk. I not-talk about hearings. [*Mad at her, he sits on the chair*]

[*JANITOR sees the trouble between the couple, wonders why their hands fly in the air.*]

JANITOR: [*to PETE, speaks orally and gets no response from him. Taps his shoulder, PETE looks up*] HANDS FLYING?

PETE: ME TALK. ME HEAR NO.

JANITOR: WHAT?

PETE: YOU MOUTH TALK . . . ME HANDS TALK.

JANITOR: [*Giggles*] HANDS TALK?

PETE: [*Tries to explain to him*] LOOK . . . [*Points at MAID*] SHE YOU MOUTH TALK . . . [*Points at MISS McCAIN*] SHE ME HANDS TALK.

JANITOR: "Oh oh oh, I see . . . " [*Points at MISS McCAIN*] SHE YOU TOGETHER [*Giggles*]

PETE: NO NO TOGETHER NO NO [*Points at MAID*] SHE YOU RING-MARRIED?

JANITOR: NO NO [*Laughs*] YOU SMART. [*Giggles*]

MAID: NO NO "No, I ain't no marry him."

[*JANITOR still giggles, takes MAID to the left center, exit.*]

PETE: [*to MISS McCAIN*] I only ask you if I can take you out with us. Have <u>fun</u>.

MISS McCAIN: <u>No no</u>. Remember what has happened last fall here. You <u>were</u> wild. I was-embarrassed. You <u>even</u> screamed and hearings everybody looked-at-you. I swear I would never go out with you again.

PETE: Hearings looked-at-me <u>so</u> <u>what</u>. They made noises same. <u>Ok</u>. You still stubborn. Worry what hearings think about you. Worry/worry. <u>Ok</u>. I will still have <u>fun</u>.

[*TERRY and VITO enter from the hotel front.*]

VITO: Successful?

PETE: She won't.

TERRY: See. I told you. I know you fail.
VITO: Fuck! [*to PETE*] Try one more. If fail, why not go out ourselves.

TERRY: If you ask, you will fail.

VITO: Fuck!

PETE: Shut-up! Always say fail/fail.

TERRY: True <u>fact</u>. I know. [*Crosses to MISS McCAIN, turns to boys*] Woman funny mind.

VITO: Always think fail/fail. Finish!

PETE: Finish! I tired. Always talk/talk fail. I bored.

TERRY: Everyone you always think plan/plan, find way fool people.

PETE: Shut-up. You always careful/careful. Always avoid trouble.

[*CHUCK and his new girl, SUSIE SLADE enter from the hotel front.*]

VITO: Yes, avoid trouble.

PETE: Safe/safe.

CHUCK: What-is-up? Avoid trouble?

SUSIE: What trouble?

CHUCK: Quiet. Let me talk with them.

SUSIE: Curious

VITO: Quiet!

CHUCK: What trouble?

PETE: Same old same business.

TERRY: See! Business plan/plan.

CHUCK: Woman still refuse let you?

PETE: Yes. Bitch! Always shook-head. <u>Nonono</u>. Always worry/worry what hearings think.

CHUCK: I can (9) convince.

TERRY: You will fail.

VITO: [*Jumps at TERRY*] Shut-up. [*Begins to fight*]

CHUCK: [*Stops VITO*] Shut-up. Quiet!

PETE: Quiet control quiet.

SUSIE: [*to CHUCK*] You can't convince!

CHUCK: [*Raises arms*] Come. [*They come to him*] Want proof. I will show you. [*to SUSIE*] You go flatter . . . say "I just arrive" ask "please go with me, I afraid of boys." You know how.

[*MISS McCAIN exits quietly to the hotel front. ALICE enters upright.*]

SUSIE: <u>Ok</u> for your <u>sake</u>.

[*GANG finds MISS McCAIN gone and are surprised to see ALICE.*]

CHUCK: Hello.

ALICE: Hello.

VITO: Beautiful!

TERRY: Lady!

PETE: Body-figure!

CHUCK: Why you left us. Ran-away from us.

ALICE: I went to . . . to school.

SUSIE: [*to CHUCK*] Who. [*Points at ALICE*] Who/who.

CHUCK: [*Ignores SUSIE, to ALICE*] <u>No</u> you didn't. I heard you moved to <u>apt</u> plushy, lived with man. Right?

SUSIE: [*to VITO*] Who/who?

VITO: <u>Alice</u>.

CHUCK: Why you ignore us?

SUSIE: [*to CHUCK*] Your girl friend before?

CHUCK: Shut-up. I not ask you ask me!

ALICE: [*Tries to calm him, to SUSIE*] I <u>am</u> <u>Alice</u> <u>Babel</u>.

SUSIE: [*Acts shy, TERRY urges her to tell her name*]
My name first <u>Susie</u>, last <u>Slade</u>.

VITO: [*to ALICE*] Sign <u>S</u> (*S on cheek*)

ALICE: How <u>do</u> you <u>do</u>?

SUSIE: [*Puzzled*] Fine. [*TERRY and VITO cover their faces*]
You deaf?

ALICE: Yes.

CHUCK: [*to ALICE*] Where . . . How <u>do</u> you <u>do</u>? Where you learn?
High manners. What for! Sentence belong to Hearings!

VITO: [*Cuts in*] Why not go some place eat all-us together.

ALICE: <u>No</u> thank you.

VITO: Plan fall-down.

TERRY: Fail.

CHUCK: Why you here. With fancy gown.

ALICE: I went to <u>the</u> <u>ball</u>. I met <u>the</u> First <u>Lady</u> . . .

SUSIE: First <u>Lady</u>?

VITO: <u>U</u>.<u>S</u>. President's wife.

ALICE: Really thrilled. I kept thinking <u>of</u> <u>the</u> dance. I couldn't
sleep . . . I thought <u>it</u> <u>was</u> nice <u>to</u> go to <u>the</u> <u>club</u> and see
my friends. I <u>was</u> surprised see you all here. I have not
seen you for long time.

CHUCK: You have no friends! They know you want live with
different people.

70

ALICE: [*Being hurt*] Not true . . . I went to school . . . learn
more . . . about life . . . world . . . where people live . . .

PETE: [*Waves*] Never heard school in apt (*apartment*)
never heard.

CHUCK: Quiet. [*to ALICE*] You will learn more from us. [*Laughs*]
You not interested in us. That all.

ALICE: [*Being lost*] Look . . . I will not stay with Dr. Zeno . . .
No no more . . . I want live my-own life. I don't-know
where I will be. I want tell you that . . . I will go away.

CHUCK: Why sad talk. Simple say bye.

SUSIE: [*Runs to CHUCK*] Not nice!

TERRY: [*Tries to cover up*] Sorry. We will miss you.

VITO: For/for leaving us.

TERRY: Want alone. Want free.

VITO: OHOH (*Y*). Anyway good luck.

ALICE: Thank you.

SUSIE: Away? Far? Be-careful! Men funny zero!

CHUCK: Me funny zero?

SUSIE: No you different. [*Hugs him*] Care you.

TERRY: [*to Alice*] Need help? Want me get cab?

ALICE: No thank you. I will walk.

SUSIE: [*to ALICE*] You different. You sweet.

ALICE: Thank you.

SUSIE: [*to CHUCK*] She look-like hearing!

CHUCK: [*Takes ALICE's arm, moves downstage*] True business.
You leave now.

ALICE: Yes.

CHUCK: [*Himself now*] Please. Don't leave . . . Why.

ALICE: Please understand me.

SUSIE: [*to TERRY*] What he say?

TERRY: Never-mind. SSHHH.

CHUCK: Remember our fun. Wonderful times. Never forget.

ALICE: No.

CHUCK: Take-care.

ALICE: Yes, I will [*Pauses*] Bye.

CHUCK: Bye. [*to SUSIE*] Come, go-out. [*Exits downstage right*]

SUSIE: For/for. [*to ALICE*] Bye. [*Follows CHUCK, exits*]

TERRY: Good night. Bye.

ALICE: Bye.

VITO: [*Thumb up*] Bye.

ALICE: Bye.

VITO: [*to PETE*] Come. Let go out.

ALICE: [*To PETE*] Good see you again. How <u>is</u> . . .

PETE: Fine. Fine=fine. Same/same, work/work. Life funny zero. True/true you leave.

ALICE: Yes.

PETER: [*Searches for a word*] Good <u>lucky</u>.

ALICE: Thank you. Bye.

PETE: Bye. [*Walks off to the hotel front, followed by TERRY and VITO*]

ALICE: [*Alone, to herself*] Where I go. Who I belong. Who I am. Never find right place.

[*MARK enters from the hotel front*]

People never understand me. I must force myself understand them. [*Turns to exit, meets MARK*] What <u>are</u> you doing?

MARK: Nothing. What <u>are</u> you doing?

ALICE: Nothing.

MARK: [*Silence for a few seconds*] We have met several times before. Yes, at <u>the</u> convention. I bumped you . . . you really mad. But tonight you look lady charming.

ALICE: Thank You.

MARK: I . . . I came here . . . yes, I know you stay here . . . Where <u>is</u> <u>Dr</u>. <u>Zeno</u>? He should not leave you here alone.

ALICE: [Looks at his signing] Why/why. You sign different to me . . . different to others. Me, too. Why/why. Many people sign different. Why/why.

MARK: I understand what you mean. I like <u>the</u> real you. I remember I saw you here last fall and then at <u>Dr</u>. <u>Zeno's</u> . . .

ALICE: [*Cuts in*] Don't talk about him.

MARK: What matter. You <u>upset</u>?

ALICE: Never-mind.

MARK: Matter/matter. <u>Upset</u>?

ALICE: [*Recognizes his signing*] Matter/matter. <u>Upset</u>? You and I sign same. I thought you sign different. I saw you sign English to others. Not to me. Yes, I sign English to <u>Dr</u>. <u>Zeno</u>. <u>English</u>. <u>English/English</u>. [*Turns away*]

MARK: [*Gets her attention*] You know that many/many deaf sign like you.

ALICE: English Sign?

MARK: <u>No no</u>. Your real deaf Sign.

ALICE: What you think? Deaf Sign or English Sign. I confused.

MARK: <u>Be</u> yourself. Sign what you want. Sign to me like you always. Sign English for others.

ALICE: Others? Who <u>are</u> others? They not deaf. I use English Sign. Right? Why there have deaf tops always English. Why not follow us. I must give-up my real Sign. Sign bad?

MARK: No, I sign different to hearings because they never understand our real Sign. They have-to <u>be</u> deaf <u>to</u> understand.

ALICE: You have-to <u>be</u> deaf <u>to</u> understand.

MARK: Yes, you have-to <u>be</u> deaf <u>to</u> understand.

ALICE: What is it like to-comprehend?
Some nimble fingers that paint-the scene,
And make you smile and feel serene.
With the . . .

MARK: . . . "   " . . .

ALICE: . . . spoken word of the moving-hand

MARK: That makes you . . .

BOTH: part of-the-world at-large. You have-to <u>be</u> deaf <u>to</u> understand.

MARK: What is-it like to "hear" a-hand?

ALICE: Yes, you have-to <u>be</u> deaf <u>to</u> understand!

MARK: Yes.

ALICE: [*Pauses*] What about <u>Dr</u>. <u>Zeno</u>?

MARK: He likes English better. Think he smart. Have-to because want live in hearing world. If he used Deaf Sign, Hearings not accept him.

ALICE: I know. But many deaf people all-over I know not stupid. Bad English . . . can't help but still smart . . . even better than many hearings.

MARK: Hearings labeled us Deaf. Period. No argument. But still Deaf use Sign!

ALICE: I will show world what I-am. I not ashamed. I have learned become different person . . . not lady. I lady? No, just another person. I will not be myself again.

MARK: In way, I glad you met Dr. Zeno. If it were-not for that, I would not have-met you.

ALICE: Which group I belong. Many groups. This-and-this-and-this.

MARK: I know which one.

ALICE: Which?

MARK: Ours . . . real group.

ALICE: [Thinks to herself] Daffodils.

MARK: What? Flowers?

ALICE: [Pauses] I remember . . . at Ball . . . you-were there. I saw you . . . I began feel there must have another world . . . I tried think one word . . . I couldn't . . . but I still had that thought . . . strange feeling . . . it-is like when all-at-once I saw a-crowd, a-host-of daffodils . . . that-was when I entered Ballroom, I felt awful when I saw you stand over-there . . . left you alone.

MARK: I not over-there alone. I here. See me.

ALICE: Yes, you.

MARK: Nothing for me except you.

ALICE: Yes, you.

MARK: Everywhere you go, I will-be near you.

ALICE: You and me . . . real group . . . new world.

MARK: Only you and me.

ALICE: You and me . . . [Gently embraces him, then slowly pushes him away]

MARK: What matter.

ALICE: I must think. Many things in my mind.

MARK: Yes, I know. You tired. You need good rest. May I take you up?

ALICE: <u>No</u>, I not going-up.

MARK: What! Something happened?

ALICE: Yes. I don't-want discuss. Leave me alone.

MARK: Where will you go?

ALICE: Don't worry. I will take-care-of myself.

MARK: I will take-care-of you. Please let me take you out . . . now!

ALICE: [*slowly*] Yes . . . I am-going-up get my things.

MARK: I will get my car.

ALICE: I will meet you in front.

MARK: Yes . . . don't stay long.

ALICE: Don't stay long.

MARK: No. See you soon [*Moves to right*]

ALICE: Bye . . . see you . . . wait! [*MARK comes to her*]
Your name sign?

MARK: Why?

ALICE: Please.

MARK: <u>M</u> (<u>M</u> *on chin*).

ALICE: <u>M</u> . . . "Mark [*Thinks to herself*]

MARK: What matter?

ALICE: I thought <u>M</u> <u>M</u> Uses Cued Speech M-A-R-K. [*MARK grabs her hand down. Both laugh, look at each other and embrace, kiss. MARK leaves slowly to the hotel front*]

MARK: Bye. [*Exits*]

ALICE: Mark. He and me . . . our real group . . . new world . . .

World . . . many people all-over
Each born for live
Eat, work, play, sleep.

World . . . many places there-and-there
Each for dwell
Walk-on, ride-on, dig . . . grow

World . . . many languages different/different
Each mouth for talk
Speak, write, read . . . sign?

World . . . yes, signs all-over
Each hand for communicate
Gesticulate, mime, face-express

World . . . loves all-over
Each hear for reach
Meet, understand, agree, match.

Flowers . . . each has its fragrance for smell
Daffodils don't mix with gardenia.

Birds . . . each has its voice for sing
Bluebirds don't crow at redbirds.

Animals . . . each has its ears for hear
Lions do not listen to tigers.

Who created all.
Yes, only God.
God creates me.

I-am deaf.
God gives me my beautiful sign language

[*Walks downstage right, stops and thinks. Then turns to left,
runs off toward cocktail lounge.*]

BLACKOUT

ACT II: SCENE 2

SCENE:
Dr. Zeno's residence. The following day.

OPENING, ON THE STAGE:
MRS. PARHAM is found cleaning the room, dusting the table. DR. ZENO storms in from the front door.

MRS. PARHAM: "Good morning."

DR. ZENO: Where is Alice?

MRS. PARHAM: "Alice?" (*S.C.*) I don't know. She was supposed to be with you.

DR. ZENO: Why. Why.

MRS. PARHAM: "Calm down."

DR. ZENO: Did not she send a note to you?

MRS. PARHAM: (*S.C.*) No, she did not. "Please calm down."

DR. ZENO: I will strangle her. Go upstairs and see if she is there.

MRS. PARHAM: "Yes." [*Goes up, mumbling to herself and exits*]

[*DR. YLVISAKER runs in from the front door.*]

DR. ZENO: Where? Yes, you know where she is.

DR. YLVISAKER: I am stunned.

DR. ZENO: Come, you know.

DR. YLVISAKER: Did you ask her where she is? She must be here.

DR. ZENO: No.

DR. YLVISAKER: You mean she is not here?

DR. ZENO: Exactly. Yes, do tell me where she is.

DR. YLVISAKER: I don't-know.

[*MRS. PARHAM re-enters, panting.*]

DR. ZENO: Is she there?

MRS. PARHAM: (*S.C.*) I told you she is not here. I went-d to her room and she was not there.

DR. ZENO: Damn. What am I to do?

MRS. PARHAM: (*S.C.*) May I ask you a question? Did either of you frighten her last night?

DR. YLVISAKER: No. I went to bed first. [*to DR. ZENO*]. You were still there in the hotel lobby. Did you have a fight with her after I left?

DR. ZENO: [*Pauses*] A common fight. She refused to go to bed. I only talked to her and she answered me . . . in the most awful language. I was shocked.

DR. YLVISAKER: I am-stunned. [*Sits*]

DR. ZENO: I just don't understand. She has talked things over. She admitted she made a mistake.

DR. YLVISAKER: I am-stunned.

DR. ZENO: Stop being stunned and do something.

DR. YLVISAKER: What?

DR. ZENO: I want to find her.

DR. YLVISAKER: I just don't understand it.

DR. ZENO: What could have depressed her?

DR. YLVISAKER: You?

DR. ZENO: You think so?

DR. YLVISAKER: I am going out and find her. [*Rises*]

[*DR. ZENO walks off to the bedroom, upright.*]

MRS. PARHAM: (*S.C.*) I do hope you find her. Dr. Zeno will miss her.

DR. YLVISAKER: Dr. Zeno will miss her! I will miss her! [*Walks upstage, exits to the kitchen. MISS PARHAM follows him and at the same time, DR. ZENO re-enters*]

DR. ZENO: [*Looks for DR. YLVISAKER*] Where is he?

MRS. PARHAM: [*Points toward the kitchen*] (*S.C.*) <u>Le</u>t <u>us</u> <u>have</u> some coffee.

DR. ZENO: See, when <u>I</u> <u>am</u> <u>in</u> <u>t</u>rouble, <u>he</u> <u>t</u>ries to help me.
                      [*Exits to the kitchen*]

MRS. PARHAM: [*to herself*] "My my my . . . "

[*MISS MAUGHAN enters from the front door.*]

MISS MAUGHAN: "Mrs. Parham, . . . "

MRS. PARHAM: "Oh, it is you, Miss Maughan."

[*ALICE tiptoes in.*]

MISS MAUGHAN: "Is . . . "

MRS. PARHAM: "Alice! Oh oh oh . . ."

MISS MAUGHAN: "Sshhh." (*S.C.*) <u>Is</u> <u>Dr</u>. <u>Zeno</u> here?

MRS. PARHAM: "Yes. Yes." (*S.C.*) <u>He</u> <u>has</u> <u>a</u> fit. <u>He</u> <u>is</u> in <u>the</u> kitchen.
                    "Shall I call him?"

MISS MAUGHAN: "No, no, not now." (*S.C.*) Has <u>Mrs</u>. <u>Newton</u> come?

MRS. PARHAM: "Mrs. Newton? No, she hasn't."

MISS MAUGHAN: (*S.C.*) <u>Mark</u>?

MRS. PARHAM: "Mark? No."

ALICE: My fault. [*Sits*] My fault.

MISS MAUGHAN: (*S.C.*) Don't worry. <u>Mrs</u>. <u>Newton</u> said <u>she</u> <u>would</u> come
                    here <u>by</u> <u>cab</u>.

ALICE: [*to MRS. PARHAM*] <u>Are</u> you mad <u>at</u> me. I know <u>Dr</u>. <u>Zeno</u>
                    would blame you.

MISS MAUGHAN: [*to MRS. PARHAM*] (*S.C.*) Don't let <u>him</u> see <u>her</u>. Will you
                    keep <u>him</u> in <u>the</u> kitchen. I must talk with <u>him</u> alone first.
                    Then <u>he</u> will talk with you, <u>Alice</u>. "Mrs. Parham, will you
                    please watch him."

MRS. PARHAM: "Yes yes." [*Exits to the kitchen*]

MISS MAUGHAN: Please tell <u>him</u> everything . . . how you feel why you want <u>to</u> leave here. You must <u>state</u> your reasons. <u>It</u> <u>would</u> <u>be</u> <u>un</u>wise <u>to</u> leave him with <u>no</u> reasons. You will feel much better after telling him straight.

ALICE: Don't <u>ever</u> mention <u>him</u> to me. Please let me leave. I don't-want him see me.

MISS MAUGHAN: (*S.C.*) Listen, we must get things straight.

ALICE: I know. I sorry I went to your place and caused all troubles. You phoned/phoned. Try help me. <u>Even</u> brought me here.

MISS MAUGHAN: (*S.C..*) Listen, I want <u>to</u> <u>be</u> sure. <u>At</u> <u>the</u> <u>ball</u> you <u>did</u> this wonderful thing for <u>them</u>, and <u>they</u> never said <u>a</u> word to you?

ALICE: Not one word. Not to me. Only to each other. 'Great <u>achievement</u>', '<u>Fantastic</u>', '<u>Deserve</u> <u>a</u> medal', 'Thank God, <u>it</u> <u>is</u> all over', and then 'Let us go to bed'. They did not <u>even</u> thank me.

MISS MAUGHAN: "That is a shame."

[*MRS. PARHAM enters, carrying a tray with a coffee set.*]

MRS. PARHAM: "He is coming. He is coming."

MISS MAUGHAN: "Oh, dear." (*S.C.*) Will you go upstairs and wait for me <u>to</u> call? I will take-care-of everything. [*to MRS. PARHAM*] "Be calm."

ALICE: Don't let him see me.

MISS MAUGHAN: (*S.C.*) <u>No</u>, don't worry. Remember last night you not only met <u>the</u> First Lady but you behaved like <u>a</u> lady! "Be off!"

[*ALICE runs off to her bedroom upstage right. MRS. PARHAM puts the tray on the bar. MISS MAUGHAN sits, tries to look calm. DR. ZENO enters, sees her and runs to her.*]

82

DR. ZENO: What are you doing here! [*to MRS. PARHAM*] Why don't you tell me. [*to MISS MAUGHAN*] Oh, you have news! Haven't you see Alice?

MISS MAUGHAN: (*S.C.*) You looked troubled.

DR. ZENO: Me? No. Alice does.

MISS MAUGHAN: (*S.C.*) You must have frightened her.

DR. ZENO: Frightened her? Nonsense! She disappeared. Damn. What am I to do?

MISS MAUGHAN: (*S.C.*) Do without her, I am afraid. The girl has a perfect right to leave if she chooses.

[*DR. YLVISAKER walks in, sees her and runs to her.*]

DR. YLVISAKER: Good morning. Has he told you?

DR. ZENO: We want to find her.

DR. YLVISAKER: We can't let her disappear like this, you know.

[*Doorbell rings. MRS. PARHAM goes to answer the door, is stopped by MISS MAUGHAN.*]

MISS MAUGHAN: [*Rises quickly*] (*S.C.*) Finally she is coming. I expect her.

DR. ZENO: Alice? Is she coming?

MISS MAUGHAN: No, it is not Alice. "Mrs. Parham, will you please let her in."

MRS. PARHAM: "Yes, Miss Maughan." [*to DR. ZENO*] "Calm down." [*Exits*]

[*Silence for a few seconds. MRS. NEWTON walks in, looks concerned.*]

MRS. NEWTON: (*S.C.*) What is it? "Miss Maughan, anything happened? Something wrong?"

MISS MAUGHAN: "No, my dear." (*S.C.*) Nothing is really serious. Where is Mark?

DR. ZENO: Where is she?

MRS. NEWTON: "Who?"

MISS MAUGHAN: [*Cuts in*] "Alice." (*S.C.*) He is concerned about her disappearing. Mark?

MRS. NEWTON: "Oh, I don't know." [*Pauses, looks for someone*] "She is not here! (*S.C.*) Oh, that is why you want me to come.

DR. ZENO: [*to MISS MAUGHAN*] You don't seem worried. You don't mind that she is gone.

MISS MAUGHAN: [*Sharply*] (*S.C.*) Don't be absurd. [*Pauses*] If you want to see Alice here, I know where to find her.

DR. ZENO: Where . . . my God, you know where!

DR. YLVISAKER: Where. Tell me.

[*Doorbell rings.*]

MRS. NEWTON: "Where . . . who . . .?"

[*MRS. PARHAM exits to the front door.*]

MISS MAUGHAN: (*S.C.*) Be quiet. Please sit-down.

MRS. NEWTON: (*S.C.*) What is it? I don't understand.

DR. ZENO: I . . .

MISS MAUGHAN: [*Quickly*] (*S.C.*) Sit-down. "Sit down! [*DR. YLVISAKER sits*] Listen to me.

DR. ZENO: Very well, very well. You should have told me before. [*Sits*]

[*MARK enters, followed by MRS. PARHAM.*]

MRS. NEWTON: "Mark!"

MARK: Excuse me.

DR. ZENO: [*Rises*] What do you want?

MARK: Where is Alice?

MISS MAUGHAN: [*Quickly, to DR. ZENO*] (*S.C.*) He is not asking you.

MARK: But . . . I want ask him.

MISS MAUGHAN: (*S.C.*) Do sit please. [*DR. ZENO, DR.YLVISAKER, and MARK sit on the couch*] I have seen Alice. [*All men rise*]

MARK: Where?

DR. ZENO: Where?

DR. YLVISAKER: Where?

DR. ZENO: My God, please do tell me.

MRS. NEWTON: (*S.C.*) Why all about Alice?

MARK: [*to MRS. NEWTON*] What are you doing here?
[*to MISS MAUGHAN*] What happened to her?

MISS MAUGHAN: (*S.C.*) Please do sit-down! [*All sit*] Alice came to me this morning. She did not sleep at all . . . walking about in a rage, part confused and part afraid. She told me of the brutal way you both treated her.

DR. ZENO: [*Rises*] What!

DR. YLVISAKER: Oh, no, no. What is she talking about? We did not treat her brutally. We did not say anything at all to her. We parted quietly. [*to DR. ZENO*] Did you bully her after I went to bed?

DR. ZENO: Not exactly. She refused to go to bed. She behaved terribly. I gave-d her no cause. She used awful language.

DR. YLVISAKER: But why? What did we do to her?

MISS MAUGHAN: (*S.C.*) I think I know why. The girl is naturally rather affectionate. Isn't she? Yes, she is. She had become attached to you both. She worked very hard for you. I don't think you quite realize her work. Well, it seems that when the great day of trial came, and she did this wonderful thing for you without making a single mistake, you two just sat there and never said a word to her, but talked together of how glad you were that it was over. And then you were surprised because she refused to go to bed.

DR. ZENO: We said nothing?

85

MISS MAUGHAN: (*S.C.*) You <u>did</u> not thank her, or pat, or admire her, or tell <u>her</u> how splendid <u>she</u> had been.

DR. ZENO: But <u>she</u> knew <u>all</u> about <u>that</u>.

DR. YLVISAKER: Perhaps we <u>were</u> <u>a</u> little inconsiderate.

MISS MAUGHAN: (*S.C.*) Little? <u>Very</u> <u>inconsiderate</u>!

DR. YLVISAKER: Is she very angry?

MISS MAUGHAN: (*S.C.*) <u>Well</u>, I <u>am</u> afraid <u>so</u>. If you promise <u>to</u> <u>behave</u> yourself, I will ask her <u>to</u> come here.

DR. ZENO: <u>All</u> <u>right</u>. <u>Very</u> <u>well</u>. [*to DR. YLVISAKER*] You <u>behave</u> yourself. [*to MARK*] You, <u>too</u>.

MARK: [*Rises*] What that all about?

MISS MAUGHAN: (*S.C.*) You will know more later. [*to DR. ZENO*] Remember your promise. [*to MRS. PARHAM*] "Please bring her down. Oh, wait." [*to MARK*] Will you please move over-there and don't let Alice see you. Let her talk with Dr. Zeno. [*MARK exits to the study. MRS. NEWTON rises, follows him but MISS MAUGHAN stops her. Turns to MRS. PARHAM*] "Let Alice in."

[*DR. ZENO moves up to the desk. DR. YLVISAKER to the bar. MRS. PARHAM goes upstage, exits. MISS MAUGHAN takes MRS. NEWTON to the chair. Silence for a few seconds. MRS. PARHAM re-enters with a suitcase, following by ALICE in comfortable clothes. ALICE stands at the top of the stairs.*]

ALICE: How <u>kind</u> <u>of</u> you to <u>let</u> me <u>come</u>! [*'Here-she-goes-again response from the people, ALICE descends the stairs, to DR. ZENO*] How <u>do</u> you <u>do</u>? <u>Are</u> you well?

DR. ZENO: I . . .

ALICE: [*Grabs his hand down*] <u>Of</u> <u>course</u>, you <u>are</u> well. You <u>are</u> never ill. [*to DR. YLVISAKER*] Glad see you again.

DR. ZENO: [*Cuts in*] <u>Don't</u> you <u>dare</u> play <u>this</u> game with me. <u>I</u> <u>taught-d</u> you and <u>don't</u> <u>let</u> me <u>in</u> <u>the</u> game. Where <u>have</u> you <u>been</u>?

86

MISS MAUGHAN: [*to DR. ZENO*] (*S.C.*) If you must fight, fight nicely. She won't answer you unless you <u>behave</u> yourself. Remember your promise.

DR. ZENO: [*to ALICE*] Will you answer me?

[*MISS MAUGHAN interprets for MRS. NEWTON throughout the scene.*]

ALICE: Yes, I will answer, but first I have some thing <u>to</u> ask. Will you tell me that the <u>e</u>xperiment over.

DR. YLVISAKER: Don't say '<u>e</u>xperiment'. It shocks me.

ALICE: [*to DR YLVISAKER*] I owe <u>so</u> much to you that I should <u>be</u> very <u>un</u>happy if you forget me.

DR. YLVISAKER: OH, <u>no</u>. I will never forget you.

ALICE: Thank you for my dresses. I know you very generous to everybody with money. I learned nice manners from you and that what makes one lady, right? With <u>Dr</u>. <u>Z</u>eno you see <u>it</u> has-been difficult for me. I forced become like him . . . really another person.

DR. ZENO: <u>Well</u>. <u>Well</u>.

DR. YLVISAKER: OH, that <u>is</u> only his way, you know. <u>He</u> does not mean <u>it</u>.

ALICE: OH, that didn't make any difference if I used-to-be <u>usher</u>. That everyday habit. But you see I changed . . . that what makes difference.

DR. YLVISAKER: No doubt. Still, he taught you <u>to</u> sign properly and I couldn't have done that, you know.

ALICE: Of-course, that <u>is</u> his <u>p</u>rofess<u>io</u>n.

DR. ZENO: <u>D</u>amn.

ALICE: But <u>do</u> you know what began my real education?

DR. YLVISAKER: What?

ALICE: Your spelling name <u>Miss</u> <u>Babel</u> that day when I first came here. That <u>was</u> <u>the</u> beginning becoming <u>a</u> lady. And there had many/many little things you never noticed, because they came naturally to you. Things about standing-up, sitting, and drinking . . .

DR. YLVISAKER: OH that <u>was</u> nothing.

ALICE: Yes, true . . . things that showed your thought and felt about me <u>as</u> <u>if</u> I person something better than <u>usher</u>. I want explain difference between lady and <u>usher</u> . . . not how she behaves, but how they behave to <u>her</u>. I shall always remain <u>usher</u> to <u>Dr</u>. <u>Zeno</u> because <u>he</u> always behaves to me like <u>usher</u> and always will . . . but I know I can remain lady to you because you always behave to me like lady and always will.

DR. ZENO: <u>D</u>amn. <u>D</u>amn.

DR. YLVISAKER: Why don't you slap him?

ALICE: [*Goes to DR. ZENO*] I can't. I could have slapped him but I can't now. Last night, when I met my friends, one girl spoke to me . . . and I tried get-<u>back</u> into old way with <u>her</u> . . . but felt both-us different <u>w</u>orld. I have almost forgotten my-own language . . . and try follow yours . . . yet, yours not for me. [*MARK enters quietly, goes to ALICE and she looks at him, stunned*] CCC, you here CCC

DR. ZENO: [*Jumps*] <u>W</u>onderful CCC CCC <u>W</u>onderful!

MARK: [*to ALICE*] Where you last night?

ALICE: Wait. I mean tell you about him. Well, last night I found something . . . after meeting Mark.

DR. ZENO: Damn. <u>That</u> <u>is</u> where you <u>we</u>re.

ALICE: Wait. Let me explain. We talked about Sign. I began see difference between Sign and English. I think I can do both. In my heart, Sign real mine. Use English to others. Yes, I sign English to you. But I feel more comfortable with my

Sign. Nothing can change me. I have-been attended to your lectures, read your notes, books, articles in magazines, watched your TV, I must admit I learned alot. But there is one thing that bothers me. I beg you tell truth.

DR. ZENO: What truth? I have not told lies.

ALICE: I did-not say lies. I don't-know what exact but there something missing from your philosophy on U.S.E. You must realize that U.S.E. has nothing to do with Sign. U.S.E. itself that English. Sign is another language. Your idea of having Sign Language classes for deaf or hearing. I can't call that Sign. That is English class. Where is the real Sign class. Tell me.

MISS MAUGHAN: [Rises] (S.C.) Hearing thought it was great to have Sign class but they actually did not take Sign. It is a shame when they already know new Sign-English and try to talk with the Deaf.

ALICE: True. True. Deaf not interested and some don't understand. I have heard complaints. Now about lady. U.S.E. has nothing to do with being a lady. A lady can use Sign. You will have-to go-ahead without me.

DR. ZENO: Of course, I can do without anybody. But not without you. I will miss you if you leave. I have grown accustomed to your Sign and to your face. I like them both.

ALICE: WELL, you have both on your TV and in your book photographs and also notebooks. When you feel lonely without me, you can turn TV on.

DR. ZENO: TV has no real life and soul.

ALICE: If I stay here, you will still hurt me. I need someone who really cares for me and understand me. You have-to be real deaf to understand. [Turns to MARK] Glad you here.

MARK: I thought I would not see you again.

DR. ZENO: [to MARK, angry] Why did you come here?

89

MARK: Don't interfere me.

DR. ZENO: What will your mother say if she finds . . .

MARK: Enough, I am on my own. I lead my life. I old enough I make my decision.

ALICE: Experiment over. [*to DR. ZENO, personally*] I really thank you for wonderful opportunity . . . learn/learn everything . . . thank you.

DR. ZENO: I see you have made your decision. You know I will miss you. I will say one thank you for giving me the opportunity to conduct the experiment. [*Turns away from ALICE*]

ALICE: [*Tries to get his attention*] Bye.

MARK: [*Understands the situation, to ALICE*] May I take you out?

ALICE: Yes.

MARK: True business?

ALICE: Yes yes, look my suitcase [*Points at it*]

MARK: Ok. [*Throws a kiss*]

ALICE: [*to MRS. PARHAM*] Thank you for letting me in.

MRS. PARHAM: "You go away? Oh, oh, well . . . bye bye."
[*ALICE kisses her*] (S.C.) I will miss you, my girl.

ALICE: [*to MISS MAUGHAN*] Bye . . . thank you for understanding me.

MISS MAUGHAN: (S.C.) Oh, don't thank me. Thank yourself. You have done it all by yourself. I admire you. Bye bye.

ALICE: [*Kisses her*] Bye. [*to MRS. NEWTON*] Bye.

MRS. NEWTON: "Bye bye."

ALICE: [*to DR. YLVISAKER*] Thank you. [*Embraces him*]

DR. YLVISAKER: [*Hurt*] Bye.

MARK: Your name sign?

ALICE: [*Puzzled*] Why?

MARK: Please.

ALICE: A (*A on cheek*)

MARK: I thought [*Uses Cued Speech*] A-L-I-C-E.

ALICE: [*Grabs his hand*] No no. [*Laughs*] Sign me <u>A</u>lice.

[*MARK and ALICE wave at the people, exit. MRS. PARHAM sees her suitcase, runs and picks it up and exits. Silence for a few seconds.*]

MISS MAUGHAN: (*S.C.*) <u>Well</u>, that <u>is</u> <u>it</u>. [*to DR. ZENO*] One thing I want you <u>to</u> know. Don't <u>ever</u> call me <u>at</u> seven in <u>the</u> morning. Good day! [*Walks off to the front door, followed by MRS. NEWTON*]

DR. YLVISAKER: [*to DR. ZENO*] I <u>am</u> going to <u>the</u> bedroom and pack some more. [*Picks his suitcase*] My plane leaves <u>at</u> 3 P.M. [*Exits*]

[*DR. ZENO moves quietly, looks around the room. MRS. PARHAM re-enters, waves to get his attention.*]

MRS. PARHAM: <u>There</u> <u>is</u> . . . <u>there</u> <u>is</u> <u>a</u>nother young deaf woman wish<u>ing</u> to see you.

DR. ZENO: CCCCCCCC [*Falls down on the chair*]

BLACKOUT

PRODUCTION NOTES

Characters:	seven deaf males, five deaf females, four hearing males, six hearing females
Extras:	four males and four females (mixed)
Playing Time:	approximately two hours
Costumes:	present
Props:	
ACT I: SCENE 1:	dust rag (maid), magazine, empty tray (later, tray of glasses), convention programs, paper pad and pen, suitcases, wristwatch, convention papers, notebook and pen, paychecks.
ACT I: SCENE 2:	tray of cokes
ACT I: SCENE 3:	notebooks, letters, Christmas cards, Christmas books, Christmas parcels
ACT I: SCENE 4:	notebook, tray with a glass of milk, cookies, cans of beer, about twenty comic books
ACT I: SCENE 5:	book of American Indian Sign Language, glass of sherry, tray of glasses and sherry bottle
ACT I: SCENE 6:	tray of champagne glasses (filled)
ACT II: SCENE 1:	none
ACT II: SCENE 2:	dust rag, suitcase (Dr. Ylvisaker's), tray of coffee set, suitcase (Alice's)
Sound:	none

Laurent Clerc:
A Profile

CAST OF ORIGINAL PERFORMANCE

LAURENT CLERC, 31:	instructor of the Royal Institution, deaf
DUBOIS, 50's:	cookman, deaf
JEAN MASSIEU, 44:	instructor, deaf
THOMAS GALLAUDET, 29:	visitor from America, hearing
ABBE SICARD, 74:	superintendent, hearing
CHARLES, 15:	student at the Royal Institution, deaf
MICHEL, 15:	student at the Royal Institution, deaf
COUNT ALEXANDER, 13:	student at the Royal Institution, deaf
ELIZABETH BOARDMAN, 24:	student of Connecticut Asylum, deaf
SOPHIA FOWLER, 21:	student of Connecticut Asylum, deaf
ALICE COGSWELL, 13:	student of Connecticut Asylum, deaf
WILSON WHITMAN, 13:	student of Connecticut Asylum, deaf
MRS. WHITTELSEY, 40's:	matron and wife of the superintendent, hearing
MISS LYDIA HUNTLEY, 28:	poetess, hearing

A historical drama in three acts dealing

with Laurent Clerc's preparation for America

and the dilemma of his subsequent decision.

The action of the play takes place in Paris, France

and Hartford, Connecticut between

the years 1816 and 1819.

ACT I

SCENE:
LAURENT CLERC'S apartment in the Royal Institution for the Deaf and Dumb in
Paris. Midmorning, Thursday, June 13, 1816. Right wall: tall window, louvered shutters
behind; the top of an elm tree can be seen. Center wall: plain, no special ornaments
except a cross on wall. Left wall: a door leading into the hall. Writing table and chair, 2
side chairs, couch, globe on tripod, bookshelves.

OPENING, ON THE STAGE:
Darkened room. LAURENT CLERC enters the door, crossing to the window. He opens
the window and throws open the shutters. Sunlight streams through the room, illumi-
nating it. DUBOIS enters with CLERC's suitcases.

DUBOIS: [*Places the suitcases near the writing table.*] Any more?

CLERC: No. Thank you.

DUBOIS: Arrived early! I surprised. Always change your mind. Went to cities. Then to many offices. Then on business trip. Back and forth.

CLERC: Yes. I am always busy.

DUBOIS: Something happened? Before you calm. Traveled little. Now more.

CLERC: Yes. More.

DUBOIS: You left Paris two weeks ago on June 1st for home. I thought your vacation. 12 days later you came back here. Lyon really far.

CLERC: Help me carry the trunk.

DUBOIS: [*Puzzled by his non-response*] Carry to where? [*Helps him bring up the trunk: stops and stares at the trunk.*] You go away again?

CLERC: Yes.

97

DUBOIS: Trunk not mean traveling. It means moving. You move?

CLERC: Yes . . . for a while.

DUBOIS: Where? [*Pauses*] England? Move to England again?

CLERC: No, not to England.

DUBOIS: [*Still puzzled*] Germany?

CLERC: No. I am going to America.

DUBOIS: America? Where?

CLERC: Far away from France. Across the Atlantic ocean.

DUBOIS: [*Pause*] You mean, Indians.

CLERC: [*Accepts his word.*] Yes.

DUBOIS: [*Dumbfounded*] You teach deaf and dumb Indians?

CLERC: Maybe. I don't know.

DUBOIS: When will you go to America?

CLERC: Tomorrow. I don't have time to talk now. Will you please go to the tailor to fetch my suit? Rue de Jacques near the millinery. [*Gets money from the table.*] Here are money. Wait. Also, buy 2 notebooks . . . extra money. [*Gives DUBOIS extra money.*]

DUBOIS: [*At the door, turns to CLERC.*] Forgot to tell you. Remember I bought a new pocket watch . . . because no clock in the Institution. Children always came up to me and asked what time. While you gone, I went to church and climbed up the tower. Really secretly repair old church clock. Clock works. [*Crosses to window, showing CLERC*] Look!

CLERC: It works! I have been here for many years and always looked at the church clock which never worked. I am happy to see it work. Beautiful. Deaf children will be happy.

DUBOIS: Should be happy. No more bothering me.

CLERC: No, they won't be bothering you any more.

DUBOIS: Yes, no more bothering. [*Shows his pride*] Look at the clock. Hard work, dirty inside, different machine, now clean, finally perfect time.

CLERC: Wait. [*Crosses to DUBOIS*] I have my watch. Do you think it works well like the church clock? [*Hands the watch to him*]

DUBOIS: Let me see. [*Looks at the watch, crosses to the window, looking at the church clock.*] Little mistake. [*Adjusts the time.*] Good watch. Time will live long.

CLERC: [*Chuckles*] Time will live long? Thank you. Yes, time will live long.

DUBOIS: [*Not catch what he says*] Need time? Need clock? You have a watch.

CLERC: I need time . . . time is so short for me. I am busy . . . I need time to prepare . . . packing . . . [*Points to the trunk*]

DUBOIS: Oh Oh. Forgive me.

CLERC: Listen. Please fetch my clothing and don't forget the notebooks. Also, report to Gallaudet that I am here.

DUBOIS: Gallaudet? New man here . . . with glasses? From America? Indians country?

CLERC: Yes, you are right. Gallaudet from America.

DUBOIS: [*Crosses to the door, stops.*] Oh, you move to America with him?

CLERC: No time to talk about it. Please follow what I said.

DUBOIS: Sorry. Sorry. I always like you. Like help you. I run, later I back.

CLERC: Yes, yes. Oh, wait a minute. On the way, tell Jean Massieu that I arrived today.

DUBOIS: All right. All right. [*DUBOIS exits*]

CLERC: [*At the window*] For many years I always depended on my little watch. Everyday I prayed the church clock would work and everyday it never worked. Now it works and now I am leaving. [*Begins packing. SICARD appears at the door. He see CLERC at the table and walks to him and pats his shoulder gently. CLERC looks up, staring at him. He kisses SICARD's hand. SICARD is fluent in sign language.*]

CLERC: I was packing and . . .

SICARD: Yes, I know. My dear Laurent, please let us have a little time together. We need a good talk.

CLERC: Yes. Please be seated. [*Leads SICARD to a chair.*] Here. [*Sits on another chair, facing SICARD*]

SICARD: Please forgive me for writing your mother. Yes, I changed my mind and had to inform her of the danger. Did you have any communication with your mother?

CLERC: Yes.

SICARD: What did she say?

CLERC: [*Pauses*] She let me . . . go to America.

SICARD: [*Closes his eyes, speaks vocally*] <u>Forsan</u> <u>et</u>? <u>olim</u> <u>meminisse</u> <u>iuvabit</u>. [*Opens his eyes*] I didn't think she would let you go.

CLERC: Yes, she let me go . . . with much reluctance.

SICARD: I thought so. Did you see your brothers and sisters and friends?

CLERC: Yes, some of them encouraged me to go.

SICARD: Some? How many?

CLERC: Just a few. I bid my family and friend farewell. I know it won't be long before I come back here.

SICARD: Three years is long for our dear children. Our deaf and dumb children.

CLERC: Please let me go. Don't be sad hearted. You taught me to be kind to unfortunate children. There are more unfortunate children in America.

SICARD: You were born in the Catholic religion, and you wish to go to a country where they do not believe in our religion.

CLERC: I will always believe in Catholicism.

SICARD: You will teach children in the Protestant religion, whose ministers are not true minister.

CLERC: I will not lose my faith. You have taught me. Two weeks ago I called on Viconte de Montmorency. He gave me his approval as did M. de Gerando. He required that I should remain faithful to my religion, to my country, to my king. I have promised this. I renew the promise more specially to you.

SICARD: But my good child, will you indeed be firm in the religion which I have taught you?

CLERC: Yes.

SICARD: Can I trust your promise?

CLERC: Yes.

SICARD: Can I depend on this essential point?

CLERC: Yes.

SICARD: Will you be faithful following rules of our religion?

CLERC: I will follow them.

SICARD: In the new country, will you remember all holy days?

CLERC Yes, I will not forget them.

SICARD: Will you eat meat on Fridays and Saturdays? Answer my questions.

CLERC: Alas, it is too late to give up the journey. My fare to Havre was paid. Gallaudet already bought ship tickets for us. I have ordered clothing. The tailor has already cut them out and they should be ready. I just sent Dubois to get them.

SICARD: You will save more money if you stay.

CLERC: Today I will sign the contract for a salary of 2500 francs with board, lodging, washing, fires and lights. They are all in the contract. After three years engagement I shall be free to return to France with an award of 7500 francs.

SICARD: Here you will earn more money.

CLERC: Last spring I wrote a letter to the Directors asking for a raise and I have been here 8 years and my salary has not been increased a single sou.

SICARD: I am sorry for delaying but your salary will be increased.

CLERC: No. I shall have the pleasure of seeing that beautiful country . . . America, and of acquiring valuable knowledge.

SICARD: We need you for the demonstrations. Many people have been amazed by your answers to their profound questions. I am concerned about your absence.

CLERC: You have given many permissions to hearing teachers. I hope you will give me your permission as well.

SICARD: [*Pause*] You have my permission. You may go and I go another way. I will write a letter to Bishop Cheverus of Boston to introduce you. Give me your hands and I pray for your courage.

CLERC: I pray God to grant you the strength for this cruel parting.

SICARD: I have always had my strength. My dear Laurent, you are truly the Apostle for the Deaf and Dumb in the New World.

CLERC: Thank you.

SICARD: I give my blessing on your transatlantic crossing. Au revoir!

CLERC: May I pray with you tomorrow morning before I leave?

SICARD: Yes, my dear child.

[*SICARD exits.*]

CLERC: [*Moves to the window, looking at the clock.*] Oh, my God. Please help me. I just could not make up my mind. I have been strong ever since Gallaudet asked me. [*Moves around*] Did I make a right decision? [*Walks back and forth.*] Sicard does not think I do right. Can't I lead my own life? I need freedom. Yes, I know they need me here. Yes, I know there are many unfortunate beings in the world. I want to help Americans but I cannot forsake my pupils. Please forgive me for my agony. I need your help. Give me strength. [*Resumes packing business. The door opens slowly and the arm of a man appears, waving a handkerchief. CLERC turns, noticing the waving handkerchief and walks to the door and opens it.*]

CLERC: Come in. [*JEAN MASSIEU enters*] Dubois told you that I got here?

MASSIEU: No, I always check your room.

CLERC: [*Notices MASSIEU's new vest*] A new vest? You have bought from the antique clothes store?

MASSIEU: Yes . . . you had a nice trip?

CLERC: Yes, but it was a short vacation.

MASSIEU: How is your mother?

CLERC: Fine as always.

MASSIEU: Brothers and sisters?

CLERC: Fine.

MASSIEU: Relations?

CLERC: Fine. You know why I went home?

MASSIEU: Yes. Yes. I hate to ask you in the beginning.

CLERC: I know.

MASSIEU: What is . . . what is your mother's decision?

CLERC: My mother's decision? No, my own decision. I only asked for her consent.

MASSIEU: Yes, her consent. She won't let you go to America?

CLERC: She did not like the idea of my going to a strange land. I had a long talk, trying to convince her. She still did not approve it. Several people agreed with me, but not my mother.

MASSIEU: So you decided to stay here?

CLERC: No! I finally made my mother to approve it with reluctance.

MASSIEU: I don't blame her. I would have the same response as your mother.

CLERC: Everyone does. After talking with Sicard, I went home and expected to surprise mother. It was not a vacation time. I entered the door and saw my mother sitting by the fireplace, starring at the hearth. She slowly turned to me, looking calm and then nodded. And I wrote, "You expected me?" She said, "Yes." and then she looked back at the fireplace. I walked to her, knelt and looked at her. She wrote, "I received a letter from Sicard."

MASSIEU: A letter from Sicard?

CLERC: Yes, it got there before me.

MASSIEU: Writing about what?

CLERC: What would you write in the letter if you were Sicard? Sicard has changed his mind and asked my mother to refuse her consent; saying he "could not spare me!"

MASSIEU: Before you went home, did he agree with you?

CLERC: Yes, after several days of talking and even writing letters to him, he agreed with me.

MASSIEU: I doubt he willingly agreed with you.

CLERC: I know he was heartbroken.

MASSIEU: Yes, of course. [*Checks his pocket watch*] How could he let you go? After seven years in school as his favorite pupil and then 8 years teaching here. Could he simply say, "Yes, my dear child, you may go to America?"

CLERC: But I need my freedom. Nobody will lead my life for me. Nobody will tell me what to do.

MASSIEU: You have always said.

CLERC: Listen, I was appointed to go to Russia . . . That was all planned until the very last minute when it had to be called off. I lost a wonderful opportunity.

MASSIEU: It was not Sicard's fault.

CLERC: No, but I still lost that chance. Now I won't lose the opportunity of going to America.

MASSIEU: You won't lose anything if you stay in France.

CLERC: Only three years in America! That is the best opportunity I could ever have in the world. I could not find anything like that in France! After three years, I shall return here.

MASSIEU: I heard that in America, there is terrible climate, the diseases . . . yellow fever. You may die in an unknown land. You are 31 years old, only half way to death. Don't go and die in America.

CLERC: You are 44 years old . . . nearly dead already, and all your years are the same.

MASSIEU: [*Resists*] I am here to teach deaf and dumb children. French children! Yes, I am truly French. I was born French, I live French, and I shall die French.

CLERC: What is the matter with you? I said I will be in America for only 3 years. I will live and die a Frenchman just like you.

MASSIEU: You are a traitor to the deaf French. Don't forget the French revolution. They died for France.

CLERC: What are you trying to tell me the French revolution has nothing to do with me going to America. Many great men have left France for a time and then returned to France. Napoleon, for instance.

MASSIEU: Yes, he did but he did not stay very long.

CLERC: He would have stayed if he could. The King returned, too. Even Sicard returned from England. All true Frenchmen returned to France. I shall return to France.

MASSIEU: [*Checks his second pocket watch*] Why waste your time in a young country? Paris is 2000 years old and America is only 40 years old. Paris is the foremost city of the world.

CLERC: Rome is older than Paris and where is the Rome?

MASSIEU: Don't argue about the ages of cities . . .

CLERC: I did not argue with you; it was you who started.

MASSIEU: Please. Remember the war of 1812. England and America at war. You may be caught in another war. You may be caught in another war between America and England . . . maybe France.

CLERC: America and France are on good terms. Why should they fight each other?

MASSIEU: One more thing that may be difficult for you. It is . . . the language . . . a new language that you have to learn. French is your language and you don't know know English. How could you dare to go to America without knowing one English word?

CLERC: I know some English, What will I do on the ship? I will study more English with the help of Gallaudet. He promised me. In return for his kindness, I will teach him our sign language.

MASSIEU: So that you can teach Indians.

CLERC: Maybe a few Indians. Gallaudet said there were not as many Indians as before.

ACT I

MASSIEU: Maybe you have to teach wild boys like the Wild Boy from Aveyron.

CLERC: Maybe I will teach them better than Dr. Itard.

MASSIEU: Stop. Frankly, it is you we are all concerned about.

CLERC: You will not be concerned when I return to France.

MASSIEU: You may be a broken man. America will throw you down in the gutter.

CLERC: I simply get up and walk. I can always come back to France.

MASSIEU: Oh, you are just as stubborn as ever. Never change.

CLERC: Look who is talking. You are stubborn, too.

MASSIEU: Enough. Go your way.

CLERC: I don't want to fight with you. You are always my friend. We have been together for a long time.

MASSIEU: Please don't talk about it.

CLERC: Please. You have helped me. You are a genius. You have taught me to believe in my own judgments. You have taught me to see the world. [Smiles] If it were not for you, I would have no idea what America was. It was you who taught me.

MASSIEU: Don't be ridiculous. I never taught you how to go America.

CLERC: [Laughs] You have already taught me!

MASSIEU: Listen, you are single. Who will take care of you? You are not even married.

CLERC: I never thought of it. Well, it is better to go to America while I am still a bachelor.

MASSIEU: Why don't you get married? Here in France. Then you won't have to worry.

CLERC: Three years is not that long. When I get back here, I may get married.

107

MASSIEU: By the time you get back, all the girls your age will be married already.

CLERC: What about yourself? You are not married yet.

MASSIEU: I have not found the perfect girl.

CLERC: The perfect girl might not find you a perfect gentleman.

MASSIEU: You, too!

CLERC: Really?

MASSIEU: Please understand how I feel about your feeling. I try to remember that three years is not that long. I will see you back in France. Sicard needs you. He is getting old.

CLERC: I still love Sicard.

MASSIEU: Don't forget that we the deaf and dumb are your brothers.

CLERC: Yes, I love them. That's enough! That makes me want to stay here. Oh, I am confused. I still love them.

MASSIEU: You will love them more if you stay here. Please change your mind.

CLERC: Please leave me alone for a while. I cannot think clearly and straight. Please go. I need a little time to meditate. Yes, I need time to myself.

MASSIEU: When will you leave?

CLERC: Tomorrow morning. I am packing now and I will leave some of my belongings to make sure that I come back here.

[*CHARLES, MICHEL and COUNT ALEXANDER run in.*]

CHARLES: Liar! you Liar!

CLERC: Calm down. What is the matter?

CHARLES: I just heard . . . heard . . .

CLERC: Heard about what?

MICHEL: You know. Abbe Sicard just told us.

CLERC: It was nice of him to tell you.

CHARLES: [*Pauses*] Is it true that you are leaving here?

MASSIEU: Everyone in the whole institution knows about it.

CLERC: It is not me they are talking about. It is the place "America" they are talking about.

MASSIEU: [*Checks his third pocket watch*] Excuse me. I will see you later and let me know your decision. Adieu.

[*MASSIEU exits*]

CLERC: I was going to tell all you boys today.

MICHEL: Why all this secret?

CLERC: No secret.

MICHEL: You hate us. Why?

CLERC: No . . . no. I don't hate you.

MICHEL: Liar. Everyone knows. You have cheated us. We always loved you because you helped us greatly. Look, what is happening.

CLERC: Let me explain.

COUNT: No, you once said that you would never leave us because your heart always belonged to us. Now your black heart does not belong to us any more.

CHARLES: You are going away forever.

CLERC: No, not forever. Only 3 years.

MICHEL: 3 years. Not fair. By the time you return home, I will not be here.

CLERC: [*Surprised*] When will you finish?

MICHEL: Next year.

CLERC: [*to COUNT*] And you?

COUNT   Don't bother asking me. [*Walks away.*]

CLERC: [*to CHARLES*] And you?

CHARLES: Two years.

CLERC: Time flies. [*to MICHEL*] Will you go back to Rouen?

MICHEL: I don't know.

CLERC: [*to CHARLES*] Help your father in Marseille?

CHARLES: I don't know.

CLERC: Why? You both don't know.

CHARLES: Because you leave us. We don't know what we will do.

CLERC: Listen, we have fine teachers: M. Massieu, M. Jauffret.

MICHEL: You will forget us.

CLERC: Please. Even in America, I will think of you all.

CHARLES: Why do you go to America? That man glasses.

MICHEL: Yes. Black hair. [*Imitates him*]

CLERC: Yes, that is M. Gallaudet.

CHARLES: You go with him?

CLERC: He is a wonderful man who helps the deaf and dumb children.

COUNT: Why did he want you?

CLERC: He wants me to teach signs to the deaf and dumb Americans. A deaf and dumb girl named Alice Cogswell. I really want to help her as I always help you.

CHARLES: Without Clerc, institution not same.

MICHEL: Without Clerc, we not same.

CHARLES: You wrote to the directors complaining about the food. Now the food and soup taste better. Now who will help us write?

110

MICHEL: You have helped us. We need you.

CLERC: [*Looks at the window*] I will show you something. Come.
[*Takes boys to the window*] Look out of the window. Paris
is beautiful. Look at the River Seine. Look at the roads.
Different roads meet from all over the world. Strangers
come here to learn from us. We have wonderful schools,
fine art museums, excellent hospitals, majestic theaters,
magnificent palaces and glorious cathedrals. Look at the
church clock. It tells time. The clock is not a living thing,
but time is, like life. Time is eternal it never dies. We were
born, live, and will die. But each of us have a prescribed
time which is very short and limited. No matter how long
you live, it is still short. My life is short. Before I came here,
I spent 12 worthless years at home. I was nobody. [*Points at
the tree*] Look into the yard, there is a great elm tree, about
90 feet in height. It was planted during the reign of Henry
IV. It is considered the finest tree in this neighborhood of
Paris. It shows no sign of age. [*Counts through fingers*]
It must be over 200 years old. Yet, time short for the tree.

MICHEL: It is still old.

CLERC: Yes, it is older than us, but how old is time? We don't
know. I remember when I was young, I used to play under
the tree. Sometimes I sat down, lay down and looked up
through the great tree. The long branches spread over with
thousands of tiny leaves. I talked with the tree and asked,
"How did you do that?" The tree answered, "Always look
upward. Be proud. Be what you are. Do what you believe."
I dreamed that I would grow up to be a great swordfighter
like Cyrano deBergerac or a playwright like Racine or a
writer like Voltaire or a statesman like Richelieu. It was all
dreams but I woke up. No, they were not for me. I simply
want to work with the deaf and dumb children. I love to
teach them. This Great Elm Tree has helped me to know
my own mind.

COUNT: [*Walks to Clerc*] Yes, you think big. Decide to move. Think big, forget all of us.

CLERC: Pardon me, what do you mean?

COUNT: I won't let you leave. [*Runs to the door and closes it*] I won't let you go. Why? Why?

CLERC: [*Pauses*] Why did you leave Poland?

COUNT: What do you mean?

CLERC: You are Count Alexander, son of Emperor Alexander and you live in a fine château. You have beautiful lands. You go to lavish parties where people with high culture come. You witness many meetings where important diplomats debate. And yet you came here. Why?

COUNT: [*Proud*] I want to learn. I want to communicate with my royal family. I want to help my people.

CLERC: That is right! I want to help people.

CHARLES: But you don't go to school in America.

CLERC: No, I don't go to school but I will learn more. In three years I will return here and I will do better because I learn more just like you do here.

COUNT: [*Jumps at Clerc*] No, No, please don't go. I will tell my father to order you to stay. Please don't go.

CLERC: [*Tries to release him*] Stop. It is no way to talk. You don't know what you are saying.

COUNT: [*Pulls him from the door*] Stay away from the door. I will have my guards keep you in here.

CLERC: [*Shakes him*] Alex! Stop! You are not the same person I know.

COUNT: [*Fires back*] You have been scolding us for a long time and now it is my turn to scold you. You kept your plan a secret until now. Why?

CLERC: I did it because I thought it best.

112

COUNT: No, it is worse. [*Runs to Clerc's coat and suitcase, grabs them and tries to throw them out the window*]

CLERC: [*Catches him, floors him and locks his arms behind*] I don't want to do this, but I have to.

COUNT: [*Sobs*] I don't know what to say.

[*DUBOIS enters, carrying the package of CLERC's new clothing and notebooks.*]

CLERC: [*Helps COUNT rise*] Come, let us talk together.

COUNT: I am sorry for my ugly behavior. I never did that before.

CLERC: Yes, I know. You are upset. I know you will be successful at home. Your royal family will be proud of you.

COUNT: I am sorry. I was shocked by your news and I lost my mind. I apologize for my misconduct.

CLERC: I will tell you a secret. At your age, I misbehaved just like you.

CHARLES: You tease. Clerc is always a good man.

[*THOMAS GALLAUDET appears at the opening door, entering slowly and looking for CLERC. He has papers in his hands. NOTE: He signs influently, always looking for the right signs.*]

CLERC: Gallaudet! Come in.

GALLAUDET: How was the journey?

CLERC: Fine, but my visit was too short. I was in great haste.

GALLAUDET: How is your family?

CLERC: Great. It was difficult to part from them when I left home.

GALLAUDET: I know it is hard.

CLERC: [*Introduces by fingerspelling*] This is M. Gallaudet. [*Turns to the BOYS*] They are my boys.

GALLAUDET: Hello.

CLERC: They give you your new name sign: Gallaudet [*Sign: glasses*].

GALLAUDET: [*Sign: glasses*] Gallaudet! I like it.

BOYS: Gallaudet.

GALLAUDET: [*Laughs*] Excuse me. I am sorry but there is a carriage outside waiting for us.

CLERC: Just a moment. I am ready.

CHARLES: I hate to see you go. Don't forget us.

CLERC: No, I won't.

COUNT: I wish you the best. [*Offers his hand*]

CLERC: [*Accepts his hand*] You, too. [*to CHARLES*] Best to you. [*to MICHEL*] Same to you.

MICHEL: Adieu.

CHARLES: Adieu.

COUNT: Adieu.

[*THE BOYS exit*]

DUBOIS: Finish bring clothing. [*Shows the package*] Here 2 notebooks. Money left.

CLERC: Thank you. You keep the change.

DUBOIS: Thank you. Anything else?

CLERC: No. Thank you again. You may go to the kitchen.

DUBOIS: I like to work different places. Always stay in kitchen. [*Crosses to the door, stops and turn to CLERC.*] Have good trip to America with Gallaudet. [*CLERC puts his pocket watch on the table and takes several coins from the table.*]

CLERC: Here for your service.

DUBOIS: For me? [*Stares at them.*] For what?

CLERC: For bringing my clothing and buying the notebooks and making my time long.

DUBOIS: Thank you. Adieu.

[*DUBOIS exits*]

GALLAUDET: [*Shows papers*] Here are a few things we must do today. First, a contract. we will go to the office at eleven o'clock. [*Turns to the sound of a clock ring*] What was it?

CLERC: What is it?

GALLAUDET: I heard a bong . . . maybe it is from the church clock.

CLERC: A deaf man fixed it.

GALLAUDET: Amazing. [*Shows several different tickets*] These are for our stage coach tickets to Le Havre and these are our tickets for our ship, Mary Augustus, to New York. Everything is all arranged. Do you still have a passport?

CLERC: [*Almost forgets*] Yes, wait . . . let me look for it. [*Looks for it at the table*] There!

GALLAUDET: Don't forget it.

CLERC: No, I won't.

GALLAUDET: I could not stay here as long as I want. I left Hartford one year ago. The people in Hartford require my return now.

CLERC: They need you. I am still thinking of those unfortunate fellows in America.

GALLAUDET: [*Takes a letter from his pocket and hands it to CLERC.*] This is letter from Dr. Cogswell. Look at the bottom. From his daughter Alice Cogswell. [*Reads.*] "Come home. I miss [*Use a wrong sign*] you."

CLERC: [*Corrects his sign.*] "Miss."

115

GALLAUDET: [*Uses a right sign.*] "I miss you. I love you. Come with Clerc." Nice. She wrote by herself. An accomplishment! Oh, I can hardly wait to see her again.

CLERC: I am ready to go to America. Let me get my papers and passport. [*Picks them up*] I believe I have packed all. I will do a little packing after we sign the contract. [*Shows the notebooks*] I almost forget.

GALLAUDET: What is it?

CLERC: It will be my first journal in English.

GALLAUDET: Why 2 books?

CLERC: The first will be my rough English and this second will be in perfect English with your assistance.

GALLAUDET: In return. You will teach me sign language. What will you write about?

CLERC: This will probably be "The Diary of my Voyage from France to America."

GALLAUDET: That sounds interesting. Perhaps future generations will read your diary.

CLERC: I don't know. Let us go. [*Crosses to the door.*]

GALLAUDET: Your passport!

[*GALLAUDET exits. Clerc looks around to check if he forgets something. He sees his pocket watch on the table and walks to get it. Then to the door, he closes as the LIGHTS dim into dark.*]

BLACKOUT

ACT II

SCENE:
Sitting room in Prospect House, a temporary asylum for the deaf and dumb in Hartford, Connecticut.Friday evening on November 13, 1818. Right wall: fireplace with fireset, wood basket, irons, screen, logs, etc. Center Wall: door leading into the hall. Left wall: 2 windows with draperies–facing the east. Round table and 3 ladder chairs, Deacon's bench, writing table and chair, Bible, desk set, etc.

OPENING, ON THE STAGE:
SOPHIA and ELIZA are found sitting on the bench, reading the Bible.

[MRS. WHITTELSEY enters, is seen lighting the candle on the fireplace and moving the screen, covering the fire and the poker at the wood to start the fire. Replaces the poker and screen. Then crosses to the center and looks around and then picks up something from the table.]

MRS.WHITTELSEY: [Taps SOPHIE and says orally.] Keep this room neat.
[Looks at ELIZA] Keep this room neat.

[MRS. WHITTELSEY exits.]

SOPHIA: [Practices] Ruth left the land where she was born and went to the new land where her husband lived.

ELIZA: And she said: "Entreat me not to leave thee, and to return from following after thee: for whither thou goest, I will go; and where thou lodgest, I will lodge; thy people shall be my people, and thy God my God; where thou diest, will I die, and there will I be buried; Jehovah do so to me, and more also, if aught but death part thee from me."

SOPHIA: If it is true, should I follow this?

ELIZA: That is what the Bible says. Clerc said we must follow every word in the Bible.

SOPHIA: I just don't understand. Clerc is a Catholic and we are not. He teach the Bible to us?

117

ELIZA: I think he agreed with Gallaudet to teach the Bible and he should not teach another religion like Catholic. And what is more, there is no Catholic church in Hartford. Maybe he likes to teach the Bible just the same. I was told that the Bible of the Catholic is about the same as ours.

SOPHIA: Yes, we both believe in Jesus Christ, too.

ELIZA: Yes, he said that we should believe in Jesus.

SOPHIA: I know.

ELIZA: Let us go on with the next verse. We must memorize it by tomorrow.

SOPHIA: Yes. Only verse, 15 through 18.

ELIZA: [*Reads*] "And when she saw that she was steadfastly minded to go with her, she left off speaking to her."

SOPHIA: [*Thinks*] Does God know signs? Did you know that the word "deaf" is in the Bible?

ELIZA: Yes, I know. Isaah.

SOPHIA: Another one. I just learned from Clerc. [*Looks through pages and finds verse*] Mark 7.31 thru 37. When Jesus met a deaf and dumb man, he said, "Ephphatha, that is, Be opened."

ELIZA: I did not know this one. Maybe we will study it later.

SOPHIA: [*Rises*] It's cold. [*Crosses to the fireplace*] If you were healed to hear again, would you be happy?

ELIZA: [*Pauses*] I would rather remain deaf. I love sign language and I see more than just hear the sounds.

SOPHIA: How do you know if you never heard the sounds? They told me that I miss the sweet song of the bird, the toll of a church bell, the wind in a tree . . .

ELIZA: I don't know the difference. If I heard them once before, maybe I miss them. But to see the flight of a bird,

the swinging of a bell and the swaying of a tree, they
  are beautiful.

SOPHIA: I agree with you. Yes, it's true! You have good imagination.

ELIZA: Imagine that. We could not express our thought before we
came here, less than 2 years ago. Now I am old. 24 years
old and I wish I had come here sooner. I will finish my
school next spring.

SOPHIA: I am little luckier than you, but I still wish I had come here
sooner. I am 20 years old.

ELIZA: I remember when I first came here, I was scared when I
saw Clerc moving his hands. Now I am moving my hands.

SOPHIA: [*Laughs*] Yes. Gallaudet, too. I was confused because he
was hearing and Clerc was deaf and dumb. They came to
my house and urged my parents to let me and my sister go
to school.

ELIZA: I could not believe that Clerc did not know English before he
left France. I always thought English was his native language.

SOPHIA: Imagine that Gallaudet just learned sign language in France
and now he is very fluent in signing.

ELIZA: I really love to watch Clerc signing. Gallaudet said that
language of signs is well adapted to religious instruction and
also to any form of literature. We better use sign language.

SOPHIA: Naturally, it is very visual.

ELIZA: Clerc is a great man.

[*CLERC enters with books and papers*]

CLERC: Good evening.

SOPHIA:
ELIZA: Good evening.

CLERC: Excuse me. I would like to know how Abigail is.

119

SOPHIA: She is still in bed with a cold. I think she is getting better.

CLERC: She missed several days of classes.

SOPHIA: She always asks for you.

CLERC: I have a few things for her. Will you please give them to her?

SOPHIA: Sure. I am glad to.

CLERC: This is a note for her to read first.

SOPHIA: Yes. I will explain to her.

[*SOPHIA exits*]

CLERC: [*Pauses*] It is cold outside.

ELIZA: Yes, it is.

CLERC: [*Holds her hands.*] Your hands are cold.

ELIZA: No, I am not. [*Moves away*] Look, I am near the fireplace. I wonder if you came deliberately to give Sophia away with the books, so she could be away for awhile.

CLERC: I wanted to see you.

ELIZA: You saw me today.

CLERC: Not alone. What were you doing here with Sophia?

ELIZA: We practiced our lesson for your class tomorrow.

CLERC: Tomorrow? Is tomorrow Saturday?

ELIZA: Today is Friday the 13th.

CLERC: No wonder I had a bad day today.

ELIZA: You are so superstitious.

CLERC: Maybe so. I believe in my luck. [*ELIZA crosses to the bench.*] May I see you this Sunday after church service?

ELIZA: Maybe . . . I don't know.

CLERC: Why were you so skittish last Sunday?

ELIZA: I am sorry. I don't wish to be seen by everybody when we walk on Main Street.

CLERC: What do we care who sees us?

ELIZA: [*Pauses*] I think you have a girl friend at home in Paris.

CLERC: No.

ELIZA: Who is Elizabeth? You always talk about her.

CLERC: That was from a book I read on the ship.

ELIZA: What is so special about her?

CLERC: After reading the book, I said, "If I should ever be so fortunate as to find a companion for my life like Elizabeth, happy indeed I shall be in this world.

ELIZA: Oh, no. You dream too much.

CLERC: If I had a girl back home, I would not have come to America.

ELIZA: What is wrong with the girls in the Paris Institution?

CLERC: There are no girls in my class. Really segregated from the boys. You are fortunate to have boys in your class.

ELIZA: They are too young for me.

CLERC: Am I too young?

ELIZA: Don't be silly.

CLERC: Am I too old? [*Hugs her*] Je vous aimes.

ELIZA: Please.

CLERC: You are not yourself.

ELIZA: I could not be myself while you are here in this room. You may get another letter from Gallaudet.

CLERC: What letter?

ELIZA: His objection to having you in this room and talking with the ladies. Especially this lady.

CLERC: Oh, that is what's bothering you. If you were in another house, would you be my true Elizabeth?

ELIZA: Maybe.

CLERC: Maybe is better than no. If I write your mother and ask permission to court you, will that be all right?

ELIZA: Maybe. I don't know. [*Looks at the hall*] I feel uncomfortable.

CLERC: Do you want me to leave?

ELIZA: Yes. No. Maybe. Sophia is coming any time.

CLERC: Thank you for your maybe. [*Kisses her*]

ELIZA: Please!

CLERC: Adieu.

ELIZA: Adieu.

CLERC: Good evening, Miss Boardman. I'll come back shortly.

[*CLERC exits*]

ELIZA: [*Runs to hall*] Don't come . . . [*SOPHIA enters*]

SOPHIA: Abigail is sleeping. Where is Clerc?

ELIZA: Just left.

SOPHIA: Is there something wrong with Gallaudet?

ELIZA: No. Why?

SOPHIA: On the way here, I passed the dining room and saw Gallaudet with a sad face. Three teachers were there. One of their long after-supper conversations. Gallaudet covered his face with his hands.

ELIZA: Maybe he did not feel well. One of his illnesses.

SOPHIA: No, if he does not feel well, he would leave quietly. He does not wish anyone to know his illnesses.

ELIZA: Maybe he is tired.

SOPHIA: No, I suspect he received some bad news today.

ELIZA: What bad news?

SOPHIA: I don't know. Teachers never tells us bad news. I suspect it was about Clerc because he was not there.

ELIZA: Clerc and Gallaudet fought again?

SOPHIA: Really?

ELIZA: I mean . . . they always argue over different ideas of education. Maybe it is about Otis Waters.

SOPHIA: In trouble again?

ELIZA: Maybe. Remember what he did last month? And he was arrested for drunkenness and fighting.

SOPHIA: Maybe he got drunker this time.

ELIZA: He nearly killed one of the boys and insulted the teachers. With a knife he face Gallaudet and Gallaudet signed, "God sees." and he knelt and cried.

SOPHIA: I suspect he is not deaf and dumb.

ELIZA: Yes, I know.

SOPHIA: What has it to do with Clerc?

ELIZA: He was responsible for writing a letter to notify his parents.

SOPHIA: How do you know? Gallaudet has a large correspondence with the relations and friends of pupils.

ELIZA: Clerc took many burdens too. Poor Clerc. He came here to help to teach deaf and dumb children, not to write to parents.

SOPHIA: Yes, I know. He does too much.

ELIZA: He really cares for deaf and dumb people. He tries to keep them in good reputation.

SOPHIA: Why all the letters?

ELIZA: He even wrote my parents to urge them to learn sign language.

SOPHIA: Yes, my parents got a letter like that. He evens writes to other parents who have deaf children who are unable to come to school, to force them to learn signs and then to teach their children sign language. It makes sense.

[*ALICE enters, carrying a slate. She wears an apron.*]

ALICE: Excuse me, where is devilish Wilson?

SOPHIA: I don't know. We have been here reading the Bible and not one person came here. And you know boys are not allowed to be in this room.

ALICE: Yes, I know. He would mischievously sneak here. Mr. Weld did not come to the meeting nor Wilson.

SOPHIA: Oh, I just saw him in the dining room. He should be on the way to your meeting. Why do you look for him?

ALICE: I wonder if Wilson finished his homework? The Bible. We need practice in signing.

ELIZA: It is not my concern but I am worried about my English. I still struggle in writing a paper.

SOPHIA: I am still confused about grammar.

ALICE: You did very well. I read your paper the other day. I love your description of your Guilford House.

ELIZA: You have beautiful writing . . . very poetic.

SOPHIA: [*to ELIZA*] you just showed me beautiful signs.

ELIZA: But she has good English.

ALICE: That's because I went to school before Gallaudet went to Europe. Miss Huntley was an excellent teacher. Clerc arrived here, I already knew some signs. Clerc helped to correct my sign language and my English.

ELIZA: Do you remember the day you first met Clerc?

ALICE: Yes. When Gallaudet and Clerc arrived at my house, they found my mother and sisters . . . not me. I was at school. One of my sisters ran to call me and I went all excited to Gallaudet. I ran to him and hugged him like my father. I was not sure of Clerc because he was French. I was surprised when he signed to me and I could understand him clearly. I asked him many questions. [*Pauses*] I believe that is where Wilson is now. He always follows Clerc everywhere and keeps asking him questions.

SOPHIA: You, too. Every one of us, too.

ALICE: He does not have time for every one of us.
[*ALICE walks to the door. SOPHIA stops her*]

SOPHIA: I am wondering if your father told you anything new about the Institution?

ALICE: Yes, he always tells me everything.

ELIZA: Did he say anything lately?

ALICE: Like what?

SOPHIA: Like bad news?

ALICE: Bad news? No. why?

SOPHIA: I am just wondering.

ALICE: Why did you ask me?

ELIZA: Because we are worried. [*to SOPHIA*] Tell her.

SOPHIA: I should not gossip. But I saw Gallaudet with a serious face. All 3 teachers except Clerc were there.

ALICE: My father should know. I will ask him when he comes here this evening to check Abigail . . . I will ask him when we go home.

ELIZA: No, don't ask him. He may suspect that we know too much. It is not nice to ask him anyway.

[*MRS. WHITTELSEY enters. All GIRLS rise*]

MRS.WHITTELSEY: [*Speaks orally and sign faintly*] Dear girls, don't stay here. Alice, go to your meeting. This room should not get dirty. We may have visitors this evening.

ELIZA: Who are the visitors?

MRS.WHITTELSEY: What did you say? Sign slowly please.

ELIZA: [*Repeats, signs slowly*] Who are the visitors?

MRS.WHITTELSEY: I don't know. Mr. Gallaudet has many visitors everyday. Sophia, please pick up your books and slates.

SOPHIA: I will.

MRS.WHITTELSEY: [*At the door way*] Don't return here until after tea time. [*Reminds*] No boys allowed here.

[*MRS. WHITTELSEY exits*]

ELIZA: Whittelsey is in a bad mood.

ALICE: It is because of the cold weather.

SOPHIA: Yes, she is always concerned about the pupils and keeping the rooms warm and checking sick children.

ELIZA: Yes, the classrooms are always cold and I will be happy when our rooms change from the basement to the first floor. Clerc does not like the room downstairs.

[*WILSON enters*]

WILSON: Shh. Where is Mr. Weld?

ALICE: You are not supposed to be here.

WILSON: I did not come to see you. I only asked where Mr. Weld was.

ELIZA: Be careful. Mrs. Whittelsey just left and she may return to check us.

WILSON: Yes, I know, I saw her coming out of this room. [*Walks around the room*] She won't be back . . . maybe 15 minutes later. [*Imitates her*] "Don't do that," "Oh, my dear girls," "Please pick up your things."

SOPHIA: [*Laughs*] Please stop. Please leave here.

ALICE: I have been looking for you. You forgot your meeting.

WILSON: No, I did not forget my meeting.

ALICE: [*Suspects*] Did you see Clerc?

ELIZA: Where is Clerc?

WILSON: I don't know. Maybe he is reading his French newspapers. I left him and found you here. [*to ALICE*] You are supposed to be in the meeting too.

ALICE: Mr. Weld was not in the meeting and you were not either. That is why I looked for you.

WILSON: Always follow and check on me.

ALICE: You told me to help with your English. I was trying to help you. Excuse me, I am going.

WILSON: Where are you going? Tell Mrs. Whittelsey.

ALICE: No, I won't. I will see if Father is here.

[*ALICE exits*]

WILSON: Did you memorize some lines from the Bible?

ELIZA: We tried to.

WILSON: Clerc will blow up his head if I do not remember my part. He reminds me of Moses.

SOPHIA: Moses. Why?

WILSON: He led people to the promised land. Clerc leads us to the promised land.

ELIZA: Yes, he is a special person.

[*CLERC enters*]

SOPHIA: Hello.

ELIZA: Good evening.

WILSON: [*Weakens*] Hello. I am sorry.

CLERC: For what?

SOPHIA: [*Reminds*] He is not supposed to be here.

CLERC: Yes, you are not supposed . . . what do you want?

WILSON: We were talking about the Bible.

CLERC: Oh, that is all right. Please stay with me. [*Gives a letter to ELIZA*] This is for your mother.

ELIZA: Thank you. Excuse me. We must not stay here.
Mrs. Whittelsey said Gallaudet expects visitors this evening.

SOPHIA: Just a moment. I wish to ask Clerc about Gallaudet.

ELIZA: Mrs. Whittelsey will be furious.

CLERC: I will explain to her.

WILSON: Clerc can do everything.

CLERC: [*Turns quickly*] No. I will follow Mrs. Whittelsey's wish. Elizabeth is right. [*to SOPHIA*] What is it?

SOPHIA: Excuse me. I want to ask . . . how is . . . Gallaudet?

CLERC: He is in good health.

ELIZA: In good health?

WILSON: Why did you ask him?

CLERC: Please let Sophia say.

SOPHIA: Well, you see . . . I think Gallaudet has bad news today.

CLERC: About what?

WILSON: Maybe we did not behave. This noon some of us ran to the river front to watch the boats and we were late for dinner and missed the grace.

SOPHIA: No, I don't think he would wear a sad face since noon dinner. All the teachers except you were in the dining room.

128

CLERC: Where were you?

SOPHIA: I walked in the hall and passed the dining room. I couldn't help but saw Gallaudet. And then I continued walking to this room.

CLERC: I have no idea why he was like that.

[ALICE enters]

WILSON: What is the matter?

ALICE: I just saw Gallaudet. [to SOPHIA] You are right, he has a pensive face. I said to him that he did not look well. I asked him to smile. He smiled. He told me that he was worried about Clerc's plan.

WILSON: Plan?

ALICE: This may not delight you all.

ELIZA: Mrs. Whittelsey will be furious if we are still here. Please leave here. [Walks to the door]

SOPHIA: Just a moment. [to ALICE] About the bad news Gallaudet received today?

ALICE: Yes, not just today. He and Clerc knew all along.

SOPHIA: Please. What is it?

WILSON: Something happened?

ELIZA: Not serious.

ALICE: Yes, it is serious. You are going back to France in May.

SOPHIA:
WILSON: Leaving?

CLERC: My contract ends in 6 months.

SOPHIA:
WILSON: Why?

ELIZA: You all knew that.

SOPHIA: I did not realize that he was to stay only for a while.

ALICE: Three years is too short.

WILSON: That means we will not see you anymore.

SOPHIA: Please don't think of that.
ALICE: Please stay here longer.

WILSON: There will be no deaf teacher.

SOPHIA: How can we learn anymore?

ALICE: Go back to old days of silent darkness.
[*CLERC slaps his hand on the table*]

CLERC: Stop. Let me tell you. [*to ALICE*] Three years ago, you wrote to Gallaudet and told him to hurry to come here and also to bring me. I came here to teach you and others, too. I have left my friends and things in France that I loved . . . and I sometimes regretted leaving my native land; now you have proved that you can do without me.

ALICE: [*Slowly*] thank you . . . but what about others?

CLERC: [*to WILSON*] Before you came here, you never asked questions. In a short time you have learned and improved vastly. Listen, some of you knew nothing of written language and some of you did not even know your names. And now, you keep asking questions. Someday other people will ask you questions and you will give the answers.

WILSON: But there will be no Clerc.

CLERC: There will be Wilson Whitman! The first American deaf teacher!

WILSON: No, you are the first . . .

CLERC: Only the first deaf teacher in America and I am not an American. When I arrived in America, I said "Here am I" but it did not mean that I should stay here. I wish to go home.

ELIZA: [*Grasps*] Yes, he wishes to go home.

SOPHIA: But we have not proved ourselves as successful pupils.

ALICE: We did not have any school when you came here and you went on tour with my father. It was a wasteful year.

CLERC: I did not quite like my first year but I had to travel a lot to sell the idea of a school for the deaf and dumb to some ignorant people.

[*GALLAUDET enters*]

We went by stagecoach to the large cities: Boston, Albany, Philadelphia, New York and others for the purpose of soliciting funds for the establishment of a new school. We stayed at inns where food was scarce; we attended Meeting House where strong-minded delegates congregated; we were invited to private parties where wealthy gentlemen and elegant ladies entertained. These distinguished people were ignorant to the education of the deaf and dumb. I had to expose them to something that they did not know. I gave addresses in all the cities. Some donated money for starting the school and I was grateful for their their kindness. After eight months of hard preparation, we finally reached the historical day, April 15, 1817 when we opened our asylum at City Hotel.

GALLAUDET: [*Now fluent in sign language*] My apologies for interrupting your fine speech.

CLERC: No, that is all right. We had a little serious conversation. Forgive me for being in this room and I let Wilson stay with me.

GALLAUDET: I had a little meeting with the teachers that I wish to discuss with you presently.

ALICE: I just told them that you told me of Clerc's plan.

SOPHIA: We are worried about Clerc's leaving here.

GALLAUDET: The news has spread over the school.

ALICE: Hartford needs . . . no . . . America needs you.

131

WILSON: Can you make him stay here?

GALLAUDET: My children, you are wasting every minute when you talk too much. Save every precious moment for study. God gave you the place to work so do your work for . . .

WILSON: God

ALICE: God

SOPHIA: God

ELIZA: God

GALLAUDET: God. Pray, continue your work. Wilson and Alice, please go to your meeting. Mr. Weld expects you.

WILSON:
ALICE: Yes. [*BOTH exit*]

GALLAUDET: And Sophia, please supervise the young girls and I will return briefly to talk with them.

SOPHIA: Yes. What subject do you want me to discuss?

GALLAUDET: History. You are always good at it.

SOPHIA: Thank you. Excuse me.

[*SOPHIA exits*]

GALLAUDET: Elizabeth, please see Abigail and pray with her. When the doctor comes, please notify Mrs. Whittelsey.

ELIZA: Yes, I will. If Abigail sleeps, may I write a letter to my mother?

GALLAUDET: Yes, you may.

ELIZA: Thank you. Excuse me.

CLERC: Don't forget my letter.

ELIZA: No, I won't. [*ELIZA exits*]

GALLAUDET: Wonderful children. They are dear to me.

CLERC: [*Laughs*] Some are not children. John Brewster is much older than we are. Sophia and Eliza are quite ladies, ready to go into society.

GALLAUDET: Yes. In a few years we will have younger children.

CLERC: Next week we will have a new girl from New York.

GALLAUDET: Yes, that makes 45th pupil. We need 2 new instructors and we need some new large slates.

CLERC: I believe you have successful students—very brilliant. Look at Wilson, he is really a good student and also, Levi Backus, 15 years old. He writes well . . . he may be a writer for the deaf. He reminds me of Massieu because he always walks and fingerspells at the same time. [*Imitates Backus*]

GALLAUDET: I never thought of it. Yes, he is exactly the same.

CLERC: I keep an eye on George Loring. He is only 11 years old, begins to write poems and loves to read literature—all sorts of literature. I suggested that some of them write letters to Sicard and Massieu.

GALLAUDET: It is a good idea. I would like to print children's letters in the next report. The letters must be uncorrected.

CLERC: We should have printed their letters in the first Report.

GALLAUDET: Learning from our mistakes, we will do better.

CLERC: I hope Mr. Terry will include our discussion of communication for the deaf and dumb.

GALLAUDET: You mean different modes of communication.

CLERC: Yes, only 4 modes: natural signs, standardized signs, fingerspelling and writing. Articulation should not be included.

GALLAUDET: I will see to it that it is not included. [*Looks around the room*] We began our education in the hotel and a year later we came to this house. I like it much better. Should I say this house is the cradle for education for the deaf or is the hotel, which one?

CLERC: I think Dr. Cogswell's garden where you met Alice is the cradle. You wrote H-A-T on the dirt and Alice learned her first word. The dirt is the core of our education.

GALLAUDET: I never thought of it.

CLERC: I can picture it as the beginning in America.

GALLAUDET: [*Pauses*] What did Alice say to you before she left here?

CLERC: She wanted me to stay in America.

GALLAUDET: She put strong words in her signing. "Hartford needs . . . no . . . America needs you."

CLERC: I was impressed by her.

GALLAUDET: We hope America is your home.

CLERC: [*Pauses*] America is a fine country. I shall never forget . . . the beauty of the land . . . the spirit of your people . . . and the wonder of this asylum. I also shall not forget my country, my king and my religion. I still belong to France.

GALLAUDET: It is a long way across the ocean to France.

CLERC: How could I forget our voyage here? 52 days on the ocean. It should be shorter if I return to France on a faster ship. [*BOTH become excited.*] Remember the sailors catching a dolphin and you got the dolphin's eye.

GALLAUDET: Saw the sea monster.

CLERC: Through the storm again and again.

GALLAUDET: Rooms turned cold, then hot.

CLERC: We got sick often.

GALLAUDET: I practiced signing every day.

CLERC: I practiced writing every day.

GALLAUDET: I prayed every day . . . morning, noon, night.

CLERC: A stupid cat won't chase mice.

GALLAUDET: But the ducks chased and ate them, then we ate the ducks.

CLERC: We actually ate mice.

GALLAUDET: I remember when we were in the middle of the Atlantic Ocean, I and other Americans planned to celebrate the 40th anniversary of the United States Independence.

CLERC: I insisted on giving a toast.

GALLAUDET: You said, "May the citizens of the United States ever feel how great a happiness it is for a man to be free!"

CLERC: It is good to see deaf and dumb people made free.

GALLAUDET: And you continued, "Let us drink also to the health of the amiable and virtuous American ladies, without whom there would be no true bliss in the world!"

CLERC: [*Turns away from Gallaudet*] When is the Board of Directors meeting?

GALLAUDET: Why? What is the matter? Have I offended you?

CLERC: No, you have not offended me. I was thinking of going home. What will they discuss at the next meeting? I am confused.

GALLAUDET: I have papers and agenda. Let me get them and give them to you.

CLERC: Yes, please. I need time to meditate before I come to talk with you.

GALLAUDET: I'll be right back.

[*GALLAUDET exits*]

CLERC: So Gallaudet wishes to discuss with me. Yes, I know it is about my contract. I believe that was what Gallaudet and teachers discussed earlier. Time is drawing near. I need more time. Time is so short for me. Oh, how I miss Abbe Sicard, Massieu, the boys . . . my family . . . my home . . . I love the children here . . . American people . . . Gallaudet . . .

135

Elizabeth. Did I ever think that I would plan to stay and live . . . No, France is my home. But Alice said, "Hartford needs . . . No, America needs you." Both France and America need me. Why? What will I benefit from this confusion? I need my freedom. Nobody will lead my life from me. Nobody will tell me what to do. Oh, I am really confused. Elizabeth, it was you who made me want to stay here. You are an American but it does not make any difference to me but does it make a difference if you are not Catholic? That is what is bothering me. I have promised Abbe Sicard that I would always remain faithful to my religion. He once said that ministers in the Protestant religion were not true ministers. I realize Gallaudet himself is different and is a true minister. I am not sure of myself because of the religion conflict. But Elizabeth is truly a religious lady. I have told her that I love her but love was meant to lead into marriage? Give me an answer. Oh, my God, where do I stand?

[*GALLAUDET enters*]

GALLAUDET: Here are the papers.

CLERC: Thank you. When is the next meeting?

GALLAUDET: This coming Monday. I don't understand why you changed so fast. I believe there is something else you want to tell me. Your face looks grave. Please, do tell me.

CLERC: I am all right.

GALLAUDET: I tell you frankly that is the first and most ardent desire of my heart that you would not go to France at all.

[*MRS. WHITTELSEY and MISS HUNTLEY enter*]

MRS.WHITTELSEY: Excuse me, gentlemen. Miss Huntley is present and wishing to see Mr. Clerc. [*NOTE: Gallaudet interprets for Huntley with Clerc*]

HUNTLEY: My dear Laurent, how are you?

CLERC: Fine, thank you.

HUNTLEY: I know you are always fine. Thomas, you look tired. I heard you have not been feeling well lately.

GALLAUDET: Oh, no, I am fine. It is our pleasure to have you here. Quite a surprise at this hour.

MRS.WHITTELSEY: Mr. Gallaudet, do you wish tea to be served?

HUNTLEY: No, don't bother with it. I will stay for a short time. Thank you, Mrs. Whittelsey.

MRS.WHITTELSEY: Yes, madam. [exits]

HUNTLEY: [Removes her coat] Dear, it is cold outside. [CLERC helps her take off her coat] I had to bring a blanket. [Chuckles, puts the blanket on the chair] Oh, you have a fire. [Goes to the fireplace] My bag! [Gets it. Opens the bag, taking books and papers] Laurent, I just bought a book on Main street this afternoon. Oh, I saw Mr. Sigourney at the Phoenix Bank. He looks much better after a year of mourning his wife. My dear, his three children are adorable. I just love them. He is a good father.

CLERC: You will see Mr. Sigourney often.

HUNTLEY: No, he sees me frequently. Ah! What did I say? Oh, that book. Guess what it is?

CLERC: Another French book you want me to translate into English.

HUNTLEY: Oh, no, not this time. You need more time for yourself. Now what is it?

CLERC: You always read but books and I don't know what you want to read. I assume it is another collection of poems of Keats or Wordsworth.

HUNTLEY: No, I have too many books of poems. I like my own poems better. Ah!

CLERC: Then it must be a new novel? Defoe? Fielding?

HUNTLEY: No,no,no. It is a play.

CLERC: Shakespeare? Goldsmith? Sheridan?

HUNTLEY: Why do you think of all English plays? This is your country's play.

CLERC: French?

HUNTLEY: Yes, but it is translated into English. By Bouilly.

CLERC: Already on the market! Please let me see.

HUNTLEY: Your preface is in the book.

CLERC: [*Opens the book, showing it to GALLAUDET*] "Deaf and Dumb, or the Abbe do L'Epee."

HUNTLEY: Excuse me. Young character named Theodore. Do you know him?

CLERC: No, he left before I came to school but I have heard a lot about him. His real name is Julio.

GALLAUDET: What is it about?

CLERC: It is about a deaf and dumb boy who wandered the street of Paris. Someone brought him to the institution and L'Epee accepted him and took care of him. He called him Theodore. One day L'Epee and Theodore went out and walked in the finest and richest district in Toulouse and Theodore recognized the mansion. It was his home. It was his Uncle who threw him out and took his inheritance. Theodore won his inheritance back.

HUNTLEY: I understand it is based on a true incident.

CLERC: I am sorry to tell you, this play ends happily but in the true story Theodore lost and the uncle won because Theodore was deaf and dumb.

GALLAUDET: [*Furious*] How can people be so wicked to the deaf and dumb?

138

CLERC: They are ignorant. The basic problem is communication. The uncle did not know that hands can talk. He could have used gestures to his nephew and he would have received a most brilliant reply. Like a Chinese man I met last summer. [*Points at GALLAUDET*] He brought him here . . . right in this room and he said he was ignorant of our language . . . English, I mean. There were many gentleman sitting around here and I happened to stop by here and I was introduced to him. I began to gesture with him and he communicated with me very well.

GALLAUDET: All of us were amazed by their communication skill.

CLERC: Although he was a hearing person, he understood what this place was for and I picked up about 20 Chinese words. He told me of his parents and their families and discussed his notions concerning God.

GALLAUDET: Miss Huntley, I went to some meeting and there were several strangers from the island of the South Seas and different tribes of North American Indians. They could communicate with each other by using gestures.

CLERC: In London I visited Braidwood school, the children were taught orally and they were not allowed to use sign language. I secretly talked with them and they answered in gestures. Basically, they listen with the eyes, not the ears.

HUNTLEY: Yes, I know from my experience with Alice.

CLERC: Sometimes people can misunderstand gestures. Maybe I should say "play on gestures" like play with words.

HUNTLEY: I do not understand.

CLERC: For instance, I know one man . . . deaf and dumb who worshiped Napoleon. It was during the time of the second restoration of King Louis XVIII. The deaf man happened to look at the palace and he got bypasser's attention by using gestures. [*Gestures: Swelling his cheeks and making his open hands descend in a semi circular line in the air from his throat to the base of his stomach.*]

139

HUNTLEY: Fat.

CLERC: Yes, it was the king who was a fat man. [*Gestures: Drawing his right forefinger across his throat from the left ear to the right*]

HUNTLEY: Behead.

CLERC: Right. He ought to be guillotined. There was a general laugh from the crowd, but one in the crowd tapped his shoulder and exposed a badge of office; a secret agent of police.

HUNTLEY: Poor man.

CLERC: He was brought to a police commissary and was accused of high treason against the life of Louis XVIII. No interpreter was available. The guillotine was waiting for him.

HUNTLEY: Oh, dear, poor unfortunate fellow.

CLERC: But the deaf man tried to explain—watch me. [*Gestures: swelling his cheeks*]

HUNTLEY: Eat too much.

CLERC: Right. [*Gestures: making his hands descend from the throat to the stomach*]

HUNTLEY: Stomach bigger?

CLERC: Stomach is swollen. [*Gestures: Drawing of the forefinger across the throat*]

HUNTLEY: Full?

CLERC: This is it, "The king eats too much and therefore is fat." He was discharged.

HUNTLEY: How clever?

GALLAUDET: I feel guilty because I could not do that.

HUNTLEY: I wish I could do that.

CLERC: Oh, I am sure you could. When Thomas went to Europe, how did you communicate with Alice?

140

HUNTLEY: Alice and I were able to invent signs, founded principally on visible resemblance. They were our only means of communication. Alice's school mates even aided us.

GALLAUDET: Strange as it seems. We accepted their signs, with French signs as a part of our sign language.

HUNTLEY: Oh, I remembered, after she learned some signs, one of her efforts in writing was something like, "The world–all peace–now I am glad." She talked about the winter. "Many candles in windows–shine bright on snow" Very poetic, isn't it? She also said that you were gone to Paris and begged you to come back with Clerc. She was concerned about the deaf and dumb. I like the way she wrote "teach deaf and dumb new words–new signs."

CLERC: Now she is able to master English because she can use signs.

GALLAUDET: Signs and gestures can easily and distinctly express thoughts.

CLERC: The language of signs is our mother language.

HUNTLEY: I have several poems about the deaf and dumb.
[Hands CLERC papers]

CLERC: About the deaf and dumb?

HUNTLEY: Yes, will you please read my poems when you have free time. And tell me what you think. I found it hard to write a poem about something that I don't really know. I wish I could be deaf and dumb.

CLERC: For a while.

HUNTLEY: Oh, no . . . Maybe. This poem is not my reason for coming here. I already heard about your plan of returning to France.

GALLAUDET: [Pauses] So the news has spread in Hartford.

HUNTLEY: Are you serious about your plan?

CLERC: It is difficult to answer your question.

HUNTLEY: [Takes papers out of her bag] Here are some more papers.
[Hands them to him]

141

CLERC: [*Puzzled*] What is it? [opens folded papers] All blank!

HUNTLEY: Yes, and I also have 2 pencils.

CLERC: [*Quickly*] I see, you wish to talk to me alone?

HUNTLEY: That is right! The news of your plans has reached me and it is my privilege to come here wishing to communicate with you.

GALLAUDET: I see you do not wish me to stay here so I am retiring. [*Stops at doorway*] When you need my assistance, call me.

HUNTLEY: Oh, no. I don't think I need you. We both can communicate. [*Shows papers and pencils*].

GALLAUDET: Yes. Excuse me. bye.

[*GALLAUDET exits*]

HUNTLEY: [*Gestures and speaks*] Are you happy to go back home?

CLERC: [*Gestures*] Yes, well . . . I don't know.

HUNTLEY: [*Gestures and speaks*] What is the matter?

CLERC: [*Gestures*] Nothing.

HUNTLEY: Are you in love?

[*CLERC does not answer as HUNTLEY begins to write*]

BLACKOUT

ACT III

SCENE:
[Same as Act II. Sitting room in Prospect Street House in Hartford, four months later. Wednesday noon, March 10, 1819.]

OPENING, ON THE STAGE:
ELIZA is sitting by the writing table and is reading a letter. CLERC walks back and forth.

ELIZA: (*Spells*) Render.

CLERC: Give. [*ELIZA continues reading*]

ELIZA: (*Spells*) Esteem?

CLERC: Worth . . . value. [*ELIZA finishes reading*]

ELIZA: I could not believe my cousin would write to you. That long letter.

CLERC: I think it is a nice letter.

ELIZA: I think you should tell Gallaudet.

CLERC: No, not now.

ELIZA: Please. I am afraid he may suspect your plans.

CLERC: Not my plans but ours. It is not the right time to tell him.

ELIZA: What is holding you?

CLERC: [*Pauses*] I have not heard from Sicard. I am rather concerned by his long silence. He is getting old . . . 77 years old. What will he say of my changing plans.

ELIZA: It is your decision.

CLERC: I am afraid the Paris Institution will not be the same. They need a new successor . . . a good abbe like Sicard or a good man like Gallaudet.

ELIZA: Do you wish to go home?

143

CLERC: Yes, I do but at the same time I don't.

ELIZA: Maybe we have to postpone our plan?

CLERC: No. Well, I wish to see my brothers and sisters and I want to know how things are since mother died. I wish to see her burial site.

ELIZA: I know it is hard on you. I think we better change the plan and let my cousin know about it.

CLERC: No. No.

ELIZA: Frankly, I am scared of this plan, Gallaudet may get mad at me. Maybe even more at you.

CLERC: No, he will not.

ELIZA: What will you say at the meeting?

CLERC: I don't know. I must do something. How can I begin? Should we ahead and announce our plan?

ELIZA: About marrying?

CLERC: Yes.

ELIZA: We have nothing to fear.

CLERC: [*Looks at his pocket watch*] Half an hour to go.

[*SOPHIA enters with flowers.*]

SOPHIA: Pretty flowers. Want to smell?

CLERC: I can't. I'm nose-deaf.

SOPHIA: That's right . . . I forgot . . . Oh, I saw a gentle man outside and I am afraid to allow him in. Mrs. Whittelsey is not here.

CLERC: I will answer the door. [*Picks up a letter.*] Excuse me. [*to ELIZA.*] Continue your vocabulary practice. [*Exits*]

ELIZA: Let us practice. I like Gallaudet's new book.

SOPHIA: He looks worried.

ELIZA: Maybe he has many things on his mind.

SOPHIA: Gallaudet, too. Oh, I saw him today and I waved at him and he smiled back at me. I think he is cute. He looks better. On account of the coming spring, I think.

ELIZA: You like him?

SOPHIA: My family loves him. Come, let us wash our hands before dinner.

ELIZA: Does he still visit your family?

SOPHIA: No, once in a while. When he came to my house, I was nervous and I ran and changed to my best dress.

ELIZA: Why did you do that?

SOPHIA: I don't want to look like a pupil.

ELIZA: Oh, no, no matter what dress you wear, you are a lady. Do you love him?

SOPHIA: [*Surprised*] We are not supposed to talk about love. Gallaudet does not permit it. Let us go out.

ELIZA: I think I need to talk with you. I want to share with you.

SOPHIA: What is the matter?

ELIZA: It is about Clerc.

SOPHIA: About your practice in vocabulary. Is he mad at you for not memorizing words?

ELIZA: No. No. We just had a serious conversation.

SOPHIA: Before I came in?

ELIZA: Yes.

SOPHIA: Oh, I am sorry to bother you. What did he talk about? Oh, about his plan of returning to France.

ELIZA: Well, it is part of it. What I want to tell you is about me.

SOPHIA: You mean your plan? [*WILSON enters*]

ELIZA: Shh. [*to WILSON*] what do you want?

WILSON: Where is Clerc?

SOPHIA: He just left and he may return here and he will scold you for being here.

WILSON: I have a good reason. I have a message for Mr. Clerc. [*Shows a paper*]

ELIZA: Give me the message and I will give it to him when he returns.

WILSON: No, I will do it myself.

ELIZA: Do you have to see Clerc?

WILSON: Yes, It is very important.

ELIZA: And then you will ask him questions.

WILSON: I will not. Well, yes, I will ask him a question about vacation.

SOPHIA: In April?

WILSON: Yes, one month.

ELIZA: [*Accurately*] Six weeks to go before vacation.

WILSON: You already have figured it out.

SOPHIA: May is a nice month. My sister and I will stay in Guilford for a whole month.

WILSON: And then come back in June. It will be a hot summer.

SOPHIA: Then wait until the last Wednesday of September, another 4 weeks vacation in October.

WILSON: Yes, but we come back for the cold winter.

SOPHIA: You are always complaining.

WILSON: I will miss swimming, fishing and picnicking.

SOPHIA: Oh, my poor boy. [*to ELIZA*] What is your plan for May?

ELIZA: [*Frozen*] I don't know.

WILSON: You don't know?

SOPHIA: Go home in Albany?

ELIZA: Oh yes . . . well, I plan to . . . you see, I will finish school in April.

SOPHIA: Yes, I know but you don't know what you will do?

ELIZA: Yes, I will have things to do.

WILSON: Stay home and do sewing.

SOPHIA: Stop. What will you do? Ask questions of your village people?

WILSON: No, that is not funny. I will be in Hingham, Mass. to help my father on the farm.

[*GALLAUDET enters with paper*]

GALLAUDET: [*Ignores the presence of WILSON*] Oh, pardon me. I thought Mr. Clerc was here.

WILSON: I did not see him.

SOPHIA: Yes, he was here. He went to answer the door.

WILSON: Do you want me to call Clerc?

GALLAUDET: That is kind of you. Yes, please do. Thank you, my boy.

[*WILSON runs and exits*]

SOPHIA: Excuse me. [*Going to exit*] I think you expect visitors here.

GALLAUDET: No. You may stay here. I have something to announce to Mr. Clerc . . . and you all too. [*Takes a little black book from his pocket*]

SOPHIA: Why do you always carry the book?

GALLAUDET: It is my little calendar book. [*Shows the book*]

SOPHIA: Why it is in French.

GALLAUDET: It is a little present from Clerc.

SOPHIA: Someday I will write French. [*to ELIZA*] Will you?

ELIZA: I think so.

[*ALICE enters*]

ALICE: I went home after noon and my father told me to come back here. He said you have a special announcement now. What is it?

GALLAUDET: My dear girl, I will wait until Clerc comes.

ALICE: Will Clerc stay here?

SOPHIA: Will he?

GALLAUDET: If you went to another country, leaving your home, friends, could you stay in the strange land?

ALICE: I know, but we need Clerc.

ELIZA: I think Clerc already used to this strange land.

SOPHIA: Wait, Gallaudet did not stay in France long.

GALLAUDET: Yes, it is true. I remember. I hated to leave Paris but I wanted to go home. Clerc has the same feeling.

ALICE: You wrote to my father saying that you did not like Paris because there were many wicked people and stores opened on Sunday and many theaters opened every day. Many sinners in Paris, I heard.

GALLAUDET: Oh, no, I mean I hated to leave the institution in Paris. That is strange. Americans said sinners in Paris while Parisians said Indians in America.

[*WILSON enters, panting.*]

WILSON: He is coming. He is coming.

GALLAUDET: Here comes an Indian.

ALICE: Why did you run?

GALLAUDET: My boy, no hurry. No Indian war here. Take it easy.

WILSON: It is all right. I like to run.

GALLAUDET: [*Reminds*] No running in this house.

WILSON: Sorry, I forgot the rule.

GALLAUDET: I am sorry there are not more children here.

ELIZA: Is it good news?

GALLAUDET: Well, it is good for us.

SOPHIA: I can hardly wait. Hurry, Clerc.

WILSON: While we are waiting, ask me a question.

GALLAUDET: You want to answer by yourself.

WILSON: I want to be like Clerc.

GALLAUDET: [*Thinks for a second*] What is "rule"?

WILSON: [*Dumfounded*] Rule? simple word. R-U-L-E?

GALLAUDET: Yes, what is it?

WILSON: It is . . . a law decided by the boss and . . .

GALLAUDET: By the authority.

WILSON: Yes, by the authority and we must follow it.

GALLAUDET: We must follow it?

WILSON: Yes, we must not break the rule.

GALLAUDET: I am afraid you already broke the rule.

WILSON: Did I? What did I do? Oh, yes, I ran in the house.

GALLAUDET: That was the second rule you broke.

WILSON: Did I break the first rule?

GALLAUDET: Yes, presently.

SOPHIA: I think I got it. Yes, he did.

ALICE: Did he break the rule?

WILSON: I swear I did not break it. I didn't know what the first rule was.

GALLAUDET: My dear boy, what are you doing in this very place?

WILSON: I forgot.

GALLAUDET: You forgot?

WILSON: I am sorry but I was bringing a message for Mr. Clerc. I was curious.

GALLAUDET: Curiosity is sin.

[*CLERC enters with an envelope*]

CLERC: Sorry for delaying this time. Here is two dollars a stranger gave me for the asylum. [*Gives the envelope to GALLAUDET. WILSON gives the message to CLERC.*]

GALLAUDET: God, thank thee for this and it will help us. Every dollar will help grow a large fund for our asylum. What is the name of the gentleman?

CLERC: He did not wish to give his name. He just gave me the money. We had a nice conversation writing.

GALLAUDET: This is good news but I have better news. [*Shows the letter*] I just received this today from President Monroe.

WILSON: The President of the United States? He came here 2 years ago.

GALLAUDET: That is right, my boy. This is the most exciting announcement. The Congress has granted us 23,000 acres in Georgia. It will be sold and we will get the money for a new building in 2 years. This is the first appropriation from the Congress for a humane institution.

WILSON: You are famous.

GALLAUDET: No, it is Hartford the whole world will see and remember.

WILSON: Hartford is in America!

GALLAUDET: I have been thinking about changing the name from the Connecticut Asylum to the American Asylum. I will report this to the board of directors Monday. Clerc, we will have a short meeting with the teachers before dinner.

CLERC: Yes, I will be there.

GALLAUDET: Oh, how happy I am today. Aren't you, my children?

SOPHIA: Are you sure we will have a new building for the deaf and dumb?

GALLAUDET: Yes. You will have fine classrooms, beautiful rooms for boys and girls, and a large dining room and . . .

WILSON: Playground?

GALLAUDET: Yes, and also there will be a garden for vegetables and fruit trees.

SOPHIA: Is that the same place you talked about lately?

GALLAUDET: Yes, Scarborough Estate. We bought it last fall with the hope that we would receive money in the future. Now, with this act from Congress, we should not worry.

SOPHIA: Where is Scarborough Estate?

ALICE: At the Lord's Hill. It is really beautiful and you will love it.

WILSON: I will miss Terry's wharf, only 3 blocks from here. Now it is far from here.

GALLAUDET: On the top of the hill you may see boats sailing on the Connecticut river. Your favorite boat will come and leave.

CLERC: I think it is the perfect place. Like the Paris Institution, it is on the top of St. Genevieve's Hill and we could look at the River Seine.

SOPHIA: Please stay here because you will feel at home. The new place may remind you of your home.

CLERC: I must tell you my first impression of America when I arrived here. Men, streets, squares, buildings, everything was alike; all looked well, nothing appeared magnificent. I noticed neatness without elegance, riches without taste, beauty without gracefulness. I found that the happiness of the Americans was at the firesides with their wives, children and friends.

GALLAUDET: Yes, it is different from Europe.

ALICE: Will the buildings look the same as the others?

GALLAUDET: This is a small building and more children will come. A new boy from North Carolina will come. Our 46th pupil.

WILSON: North Carolina, far!

GALLAUDET: Word has spread over the country. We must thank Clerc for his great influence in Washington City.

CLERC: With pleasure I have fulfilled my duty.

SOPHIA: Influence?

GALLAUDET: When Clerc went to Washington City last year, he met important people . . . statesmen, congressmen, and diplomats. The Speaker of the House recognized Clerc immediately and he said that they both met in a restaurant in Paris years ago. He took him to the Capitol to introduce him to the congressmen. He stayed there for one half hour and they asked him questions. And when Clerc went to the White House, President Monroe recognized him from his visit to the asylum here for the exhibition.

WILSON: Did he still change the position of his legs?

CLERC: No, not at that time.

SOPHIA: What do you mean?

CLERC: When President Monroe was invited to see the performance at the new Institution, about 3 months after the opening, the President looked confused and he took a seat on the platform. Around were the spectators.

WILSON: I could hardly see the great man until one of the boys signed, "Look at the hat" [*Gestures: tricorn hat*] "that is the President".

CLERC: This has become our sign for the president. Anyway, Gallaudet and I were on one side of the President and Gallaudet said . . . What exactly did you say?

GALLAUDET: Something like "if your excellency will be so kind as to ask some questions, I will repeat them to Mr. Clerc on my fingers, and he will write an answer on the slate, to show the manner of facility of communication by signs.

CLERC: The President stared at his flying hands and then, he changed the position of his legs, showing a consciousness of the question, and he thought for a while. Everybody expected something profound. We waited a long time. At last it became awkward, and Gallaudet repeated what he just said before. The President stared at his hands and changed his position of his legs, and meditated. His philosophical face was shown, and finally he said, "Ask him how old he is." [*General laugh*]

ELIZA: Why did he say that?

GALLAUDET: You will be surprised that many people are like that. Many just do not know.

WILSON: You told them about us.

GALLAUDET: No, it is your responsibility to tell people that we are created equal. God's will. If they do not know much about the deaf and dumb, tell them. If they are afraid of us, don't be afraid to reach them.

WILSON: They always think we are different!

CLERC: That is right. Admit that we are different!

GALLAUDET: Will you repeat what you said at the exhibition last year. I believe they, by now, begin to realize who they are.

153

CLERC: As part of my address, I said to the people, every creature, every work of God, is admirably well made; but if anyone appears imperfect in our eyes, it does not belong to us to criticize it. Perhaps, that which we do not find right in its kind, turns to our advantage, without our being to perceive it. Let us look at the state of the heavens, now the weather is fine; again it is unpleasant; one day is hot, another is cold; another time it is rainy, snowy or cloudy; everything is variable and inconstant.

SOPHIA: It is God's work.

CLERC: Yes, let us look at the surface of the earth, here the ground is flat; there it is hilly and mountainous; in other places, it is sandy, in others it is barren; elsewhere it is productive. Let us, in thought, go into an orchard or forest. What do we see? Trees high and low, large or small, upright or crooked, fruitful or unfruitful.

WILSON: That is God's work in nature. But people are all the same.

CLERC: Well, let us look at the birds of the air, and at the fishes of the sea, nothing resembles another thing. Let us look at the beasts. We see among the same kinds, some different forms, or different dimensions, domestic or wild, harmless or ferocious, useful or useless, pleasing or hideous. Some are bred for men's sakes; some for their own pleasures and amusements some are of no use to us. There are faults in their organization as well as in that of men. Those who are acquainted with the veterinary art, know this well; but as for us who have not made a study of this science, we seem not to discover or remark these faults.

ALICE: Faults in us?

CLERC: Why are we deaf and dumb? Is it from the difference in our ears? But our ears are like yours; is it that there may be some infirmity? But they are all as well organized as yours. Why then are we deaf and dumb? I do not know, as you do not know why there are infirmities in your bodies,

154

not why there are among the human kind, white, black, red and yellow men. The deaf and dumb are everywhere, in Asia, in Africa, as well as in Europe and America. They existed before you spoke of them and before you saw them.

GALLAUDET: It is an act of God.

CLERC: Yes, I think our deafness proceeds from an act of Providence, I would say, from the will of God. And does it imply that the deaf and dumb are worse than other men? Perhaps if we heard we might have heard much evil, and perhaps blasphemed the holy name of our Creator, and of course hazarded the loss of our soul when departing this life. We therefore can thank God for having made us deaf and dumb, hoping that in the future world, we all will understand the reason about deaf and dumb. You can tell all the people of the world who you are and also, the deaf and dumb are a gift of God.

WILSON: That makes me feel much better. I always thought I was not wanted in this world.

CLERC: Will you discuss my plan of returning to France at the meeting today?

GALLAUDET: Yes.

CLERC: You know my contract said three years.

GALLAUDET: Yes, that is why I will report it at the meeting.

CLERC: It is difficult for me to tell you how I feel today.

GALLAUDET: Yes, don't tell me. I know you feel the same way you felt the day you left France.

CLERC: That was different. It was the parting but this situation is not the same. It is not my only reason. Please forgive me for keeping a secret.

GALLAUDET: Secret?

ELIZA: You may announce our plan.

CLERC: Yes. I will.

GALLAUDET: What is it?

CLERC: I should have told you a long time ago.

SOPHIA: About your returning to France?

GALLAUDET: Pray, do tell me.

CLERC: You kept telling me there might be something else which delayed my return to France.

GALLAUDET: Yes, I did.

CLERC: What did I say when we celebrated the anniversary of the United States Independence?

GALLAUDET: Your toast?

CLERC: Yes, it is.

GALLAUDET: [*Thinks*] Man free . . . something about American ladies . . .

CLERC: That's it.

SOPHIA: Ladies?

GALLAUDET: Ladies . . . what has it to do with you?

CLERC: [*Points at ELIZA*] This is the lady.

GALLAUDET: I just don't understand the whole thing.

ELIZA: Please tell him. Don't play a game.

CLERC: This is the American lady I am going to marry.

GALLAUDET: Marry?

SOPHIA: [*to ELIZA*] You and Clerc marry?

ELIZA: Yes, we are going to be married in May.

CLERC: After school closes.

ELIZA: One week after.

CLERC: That was my secret and tell me have I done wrong?

GALLAUDET: What about her mother?

ELIZA: I have already told her.

CLERC: And I have already asked for her consent.

ELIZA: Mother wants our ceremony in Albany.

CLERC: [*Takes the letter from the pocket*] Here it is. Her cousin wrote and explained the wedding plan to us.

ALICE: I wish I could witness your wedding.

GALLAUDET: It is really so soon.

ELIZA: Clerc did not want to marry in June or July because "J" represents Judas.

CLERC: Shhh. Don't say my reasons.

SOPHIA: You are still superstitious.

CLERC: Yes. I am lucky.

GALLAUDET: What about returning to France?

CLERC: [*Pauses*] I will stay here another year.

WILSON: Really! Really!

CLERC: Only another year.

WILSON: Fine! I will still ask you questions for one more year.

ELIZA: Oh, no. Not again.

GALLAUDET: Oh, my friends, I am so happy for you . . . both Elizabeth and Laurent.

ELIZA: Are you angry?

GALLAUDET: Me? Oh, no. You will finish school soon. You are marrying a good man.

CLERC: I am proud to have this American lady as my wife.

GALLAUDET: Let me announce this at the meeting.

CLERC: Yes, you may announce my plan.

GALLAUDET: Yes, I will. Wait until they hear.

[*GALLAUDET exits*]

SOPHIA: Oh, how happy I am for you.

ELIZA: Thank you.

ALICE: I am truly happy for you. I can't wait to tell Father.

CLERC: Yes, do tell your family.

ALICE: That means we are not going to Springfield this fall in October.

ELIZA: Yes, you and I will go to Springfield. After we get married, we will have a . . . I feel embarrassed.

CLERC: Vacation . . . honeymoon.

ELIZA: Yes and after that I will go to Springfield while Clerc is on business in Boston.

ALICE: [*Hugs ELIZA*] I am so happy . . . I am going home and tell Father. I will come back shortly.

[*ALICE exits*]

SOPHIA: Imagine you will go to that great country and you will see the Parisian women and their fashionable dresses.

ELIZA: I may buy a hat with feathers.

SOPHIA: And fine shoes and . . .

CLERC: Don't dream about it.

SOPHIA: I will tell my sister and I'm sure she will faint.

[*SOPHIA exits*]

WILSON: What will I say to the boys? Yes, I will say Clerc will stay another year. That is the best news.

[*WILSON exits. CLERC and ELIZA hug*]

ACT III

[*GALLAUDET enters*]

GALLAUDET: I am calling the meeting.

  CLERC: May I speak with Eliza for a moment?

GALLAUDET: We will wait for you. Don't be long.

[*GALLAUDET exits*]

  ELIZA: I just couldn't believe it.

  CLERC: I love you.

  ELIZA: I have been in this room since we read the letter and I was stuck in this room not knowing when you would say.

  CLERC: That is why I love you.

  ELIZA: [*Hugs him*] I am relieved. What will we do after we marry?

  CLERC: You already want to discuss it?

  ELIZA: Yes, I need preparation.

  CLERC: So do I.

  ELIZA: I need time.

  CLERC: So do I. Need time? Yes, time is so short. The Great Elm Tree has a short time too. It told me of my future but it did not tell me of marriage.

  ELIZA: What are you talking about? The tree?

  CLERC: Paris Institution has a large elm tree and I communicated with it when I was little.

  ELIZA: You always had a wild imagination.

  CLERC: It helps me.

  ELIZA: Don't dream that we are going to marry. We are going to marry!

  CLERC: Yes, we are.

  ELIZA: Will you tell our plan at the meeting?

CLERC: Yes, I will tell them that I wish to stay here another year and then I will go to France.

ELIZA: Only you?

CLERC: I mean we.

ELIZA: I am afraid by the end of another year they will hate to see you go back to France.

CLERC: We may stay there for one year.

ELIZA: One year in Paris?

CLERC: I don't know. We will see.

ELIZA: Do you wish to come back here?

CLERC: Well, I . . . yes, I love it here.

ELIZA: And then we will have a family here.

CLERC: Yes, maybe a large family.

ELIZA: I will cook your favorite dish . . . fried frog legs.

CLERC: That will be nice.

ELIZA: What else do you like to eat?

CLERC: I will not talk about the family and food in the meeting. Let us go.

ELIZA: One more question. May I see you after the meeting?

CLERC: Yes, time is so short for us.

[*BOTH exit*]

BLACKOUT

PRODUCTION NOTES

Characters: three Deaf females, seven Deaf males, two hearing females. two hearing males.

Playing Time: approximately two hours.

Costumes: Period costume from 1816–1819.

Props:

ACT I: suitcases, trunk, money, pocket watch for Clerc, 2 watches for Dubois and 1 watch for Massieu, clothes for packing, handkerchief, papers, letter, packages with Clerc's new clothing and notebooks, tickets.

ACT II: Bible, letter, writing paper, pens (desk set), books and paper in a bag for Ms. Huntley, blanket.

ACT III: letter, writing paper and pens.

Setting:

ACT I: Clerc's apartment in the Royal Institution—*right wall:* tall window, louvered shutters behind, the top of an elm tree can be seen. *center wall:* plain, no special ornaments except a cross on the wall. *left wall:* a door leading into the hall. Writing table and chair, 2 side chairs, couch, globe on a tripod, bookshelves.

ACT II: Sitting room in Prospect House—*right wall:* fireplace with fire set, wood basket, irons, screen, logs, etc. *center wall:* door leading into the hall. *left wall:* windows with draperies facing east. round table and 3 ladder chairs, Deacon's bench, writing table and chair, desk set, Bible.

ACT III: same as Act II with a few furniture pieces added.

Sound:

ACT I: chime of a clock

161

NOTES

NOTES